Advance praise for:

THE IMPROBABLE RETURN OF COCO CHANEL

"Finally...a first-hand peek into an untold chapter of Coco Chanel's amazing life."

"Richard Parker's recollections of his time as the assistant to the fashion industry icon, chronicles the untold challenges encountered in opening a new showroom for Chanel Perfumes in New York; the hand-to-hand corporate infighting between Gregory Thomas, the powerful Chairman of Chanel America, and Tom Lee, its legendary designer; and the ultimate resurrection of Coco Chanel's reputation and legend.

Parker's insights and comfortable writing style bring this industry-defining event and its era to life in page-turning fashion."

Archie J. Thornton, President and CEO, The Thornton Works, Inc., formerly Managing Director, Ogilvy & Mather Worldwide

****

"Coco Chanel's effervescent and strong personality is clearly delineated in this lively story of the launch of the Chanel Perfume Showroom in New York. After years of exile, her return to fame, as personally witnessed by her assistant, Richard Parker, was the second act in the astounding career of this fashion icon. Parker brings a sharp eye and dry humor to his first-hand account of working with Coco on the project which revived her career and made her a fashion star again."

Holley Flagg, noted New York artist

D0082606

PUBLISHER'S INFORMATION

For information about permission to reproduce sections from this
book, write to: Permissions, eBook Bakery
48 Westmoreland Street, Narragansett, RI 02882

Editing by Tracy Hart
www.editingwithhart.com
editingwithhart@gmail.com

eBook, paperback & cover design by the eBook Bakery
www.ebookbakery.com
authorhelp@eBookbakery.com
Printed in the United States of America

ISBN 978-1-938517-15-0

THE IMPROBABLE RETURN OF COCO CHANEL

As Witnessed by Her Assistant Richard Parker

TABLE OF CONTENTS

PART I *THE IMPROBABLE RETURN OF COCO CHANEL*

PART II *MORE CHANEL: MYTHS, LEGENDS AND LIES*

INTRODUCTION

ACKNOWLEDGEMENTS

Over the years many people have encouraged me to turn various memories and compulsive research into the story of Mademoiselle's improbable return and my involvement with it.

I have written a series of articles relating to other personal experiences, which have appeared in various publications, but this is my first long piece. As it concerns events that occurred many years ago, it required many helpers and supporters. Most importantly, my editor Tracy Hart, who aided my writing and polished vignettes. Also, a noted technophobe, I benefited from technical assistance from good friends, John Eastberg and I. Michael Grossman.

Several others assisted, including my writing group in the persons of Myrina Cardella-Marenghi, Enid Flaherty, I. Michael Grossman, Tracy Hart, Carol Hazlehurst, Virginia Leaper, Camilla Lee, and Jeannie Serpa. Still others include Betty Cotter, Christine Wulfhorst, Tris Coffin, Barbara Davis, Dorothy Guth, Nancy Bredbeck, Don and Nancy Hall, Archie Thornton and the Flanders, Marg and David.

DEDICATION

Dedicated to my daughter Stephanie
and "Cocophiles" everywhere

ABOUT THE AUTHOR

MADEMOISELLE CHANEL'S ASSISTANT, RICHARD PARKER

    I ended my career as one of the Mad Men of the New York advertising world, having worked as an artist, account executive, sports and movie promoter, textile executive, and fashion authority. Of all of the rewarding positions I've held, the time I served as Mademoiselle's assistant was beyond comparison.

THE IMPROBABLE RETURN OF COCO CHANEL

As Witnessed by her Assistant, Richard Parker

Part I: The Improbable Return of Coco Chanel

Mademoiselle emerged from 13 years of exile to unleash her creativity on the Chanel Perfume Showroom in New York. This memoir reveals the never-before-reported episode, crucial to her return to fame.

Part II: More Chanel: Myths, Legends and Lies

Almost 60 years of following the life of Coco Chanel have uncovered incidents either ignored, distorted or even lied about. My extensive body of research seeks to present the truth.

PREFACE

An inexperienced young army veteran starting his career, that was me, and an aging fashion icon, that was Coco Chanel. An unlikely combination, but fortunately we worked well together. It all began in 1953, when at age seventy she was asked to leave retirement in Switzerland to become the creative director for a new showroom and office for Chanel Perfumes under construction in New York. It was to be an art-filled edifice that would mirror her opulent apartment on the Rue Cambon in Paris.

By a strange twist of fate I became her assistant on this project. To make it even stranger, I had no experience in either interior design or working with a celebrity, and I spoke only a smattering of French. For Coco Chanel it was an opportunity to be back at work, using her incredible creative talents once again. For me it became a plunge into an exotic atmosphere, replete with unpredictable challenges.

Working closely with Coco Chanel was complicated and fascinating in itself, but I also found myself involved in a turf war at the showroom. The contest was between two alpha males: Gregory Thomas, the powerful Chairman of Chanel America; and my boss, Tom Lee, the celebrated designer, over their relationship with Coco Chanel. The dispute left me in a rather precarious spot, but the upside was the creation of my position as Mademoiselle's assistant. I started on the project as an abject beginner, but as time went on, my standing in the creative process improved. Eventually, the installation of fabulous works of art in the showroom became, in good part, my responsibility, thanks to the machinations of Gregory Thomas—always, of course, under the intense supervision of Mademoiselle Chanel.

Even though intimate aspects of Coco Chanel's life are

openly discussed, details of her creative focus in 1952, on the Chanel Perfume Showroom in New York, are almost unknown. Perhaps even less understood is how Mademoiselle's involvement in that showroom saved her return to haute couture from disaster. As there are few aware of this most consequential aspect of her career, I have written at some length about her New York experience.

I also discuss, under the heading of "More Chanel," several significant episodes in Coco Chanel's life which I was not part of, but which have been either ignored or incompletely reported. I learned about these events through conversations with people living in France at that time, and from decades of research.

Much of my information comes from personally working with Mademoiselle Chanel, more from Gregory Thomas, and some from others at Chanel. My good friend, foreign correspondent, author and essayist, Hillel Bernstein, provided extensive background material. He worked for an American newspaper in Paris in the 1920s and wrote about that period for *Esquire* and other publications. During World War II, because of familiarity with colloquial French and knowledge of how the French government operated, he was selected by the Office of War Information to make daily broadcasts to the French Resistance with messages containing coded information. After the war, Hillel returned to Paris and wrote about conditions there in a series of articles for *The New Yorker*. I met him when he returned to New York and we became fast friends. We spent many hours discussing his experiences: fascinating stories that opened the door for me to historic events in evolving post-war Europe. Most importantly, these discussions provided background information on how Coco Chanel fit into the history and legends of the time, both before the war and afterward.

The rest of my information was gleaned from pertinent obituaries and numerous books and articles, both trade and consumer, concerning the activities of La Grande Mademoiselle. I began collecting this material over 60 years ago, shortly after the showroom was completed in 1953, and have gathered it ever since. Putting this story together took much longer than anticipated, even with the help of many people who steered me back on track when I strayed into blind alleys.

The outpouring of books, articles, movies, and television specials about Coco Chanel continues unabated. Like her couture, she never goes out of style; an electric aura encases this icon. However, due to considerable misinformation circulated about her, I felt impelled to write my memoir and "More Chanel" to communicate what she was really like. My esteem for Coco Chanel began when we worked together at the Chanel Perfume Showroom. Although her talent and prestige put her at a level far above me, Mademoiselle's kindness, during this unique and potentially daunting early career challenge, remains alive in my memory as if it happened yesterday.

CHAPTER 1

The Improbable Return of Coco Chanel

*"There is a time for work
and a time for love.
There is no time for anything else."*
Coco Chanel

When I first met Mademoiselle Chanel, she had been without either work or love for many years. In 1939, at the onset of World War II, she had closed her atelier for the duration, but when the war ended she did not resume her couture business. Chanel's wartime romance with Baron Hans Gunter Von Dincklage, a German diplomat, made her relationship with the post-war government of France difficult, and she joined the Baron in retirement in Switzerland—a retirement that was, in fact, exile. For Coco, it meant the end of her leadership of the fashion world, as well as estrangement from Europe's aristocracy and intelligentsia. In time, her relationship with Von Dincklage faded away. Isolated from all that mattered, long years of boredom promised to stretch on indefinitely. Without work or love, life for Chanel was no life at all.

Unexpectedly, Coco was saved from this oppressive monotony by an old adversary: Pierre Wertheimer. Her antagonism with Wertheimer had festered for years. Its catalyst was her wish to create a personal perfume. Believing that a woman was not properly dressed unless she was wearing a suitable perfume and not finding one that suited her, in 1924, Coco created Chanel N°5.

To avoid distraction from her successful and fast-growing couture business, Coco asked Wertheimer, owner of Bourjois Perfumes, to take over the manufacturing and marketing of Chanel fragrances. Many in the fashion world had namesake perfumes and as none amounted to much, Coco did not foresee the potential financial powerhouse she had created. In her negotiations with Wertheimer, peasant shrewdness deserted her. Not wishing to be involved in the cosmetic world, Coco requested a small profit: ten percent of French sales.

The phenomenal international growth of Chanel N°5 brought a shocking realization: she had signed away a fortune. It was a mistake, with only herself to blame, but for the next 28 years, with increasing obsession, she sought retribution. During her years of retirement, a time when there was little else to occupy her creative spirit, she persisted, even to the extent of trying to use Nazi race laws to get her way. It was not to be, but undaunted by failure, she continued to take Pierre Wertheimer to court. Coco always lost, but after each decision, Wertheimer, a man of invariable courtesy, sent her a magnificent bouquet of roses with a friendly note attached.

However, in 1952 he offered her, in addition to flowers, everything she had fought for. It was not a gesture of charity or remorse; sales were down and Wertheimer needed Coco Chanel's creativity to help restore the pre-war mystique and prestige of Chanel Perfumes.

During World War II, Chanel products were produced in occupied France and distributed throughout Nazi-dominated Europe. To counter this, the Wertheimer family, who had escaped to America, attempted to make Chanel fragrances there. Unfortunately, these wartime versions were inferior to the original and Chanel perfume sales were merely limping along.

It was time for a radical change. With finesse and imagination, Wertheimer enlisted Coco to help bring back the pre-war aura of Chanel. This image restoration was to begin in New York by reintroducing Coco to the American market where she had always been popular. A new Chanel Perfume headquarters and showroom was being constructed in Manhattan, and he wanted her to create for it an ambiance bearing the unmistakable imprint of Coco Chanel.

Wertheimer envisioned the new showroom as a counterpart to Chanel's opulent apartment over the Chanel atelier in Paris. Before the war, upstairs at 31 Rue Cambon was an exclusive setting where Coco received leaders of society and the creative world, including the Rothchilds, Colette, the Grand Duke of Russia, Cecil Beaton, Sergi Diaghilev, Jean Cocteau, Igor Stravinsky, the Duke of Westminster, Picasso, the Prince of Wales, and others of the haute monde.

To attract a similar following in America, the Chairman's Office would feature treasures from around the world, including paintings by Rousseau and Renoir, important French Regency and Provincial furniture, Benin bronzes from Africa, statuary from ancient Sumer, and rare carpets from the Caucasus. The showroom would be furnished with a Chanel signature: antique Chinese Coromandel screens and would reflect the unassailable elegance and originality that personified everything connected with Coco Chanel. To insure that the creative work would run smoothly, the best American design talent would assist her.

Wertheimer proposed a new financial arrangement, so profitable for Coco, it wiped out years of animosity born of her resentment for the terms of the original agreement. Now he proffered her 2% of sales world-wide, not just on perfumes but on all Chanel products. Wartime royalties for both European and American versions of Chanel perfumes would be paid to her, along with other concessions, generating even greater wealth. Possibly his best offering, beyond the healing of old injuries, was the opportunity to again pursue what she valued most in life besides love: creative work.

CHAPTER 2

A Conflict Arises
Between Two Alpha Males

Although deeply involved in the showroom project, I did not ever meet Pierre Wertheimer. This was not unusual as he was somewhat of a mystery man. Owner of Bourjois and Chanel Perfumes and an international financier, he was known in the fragrance industry by name only, even to those doing business with his firms for years. Associates in his own companies saw little of him, as he rarely visited his offices. Never involved with details, Wertheimer crafted his freedom from the commercial world by hiring top people and allowing them free rein to operate, while he went off to his true love, a stable of champion race horses.

As soon as Coco became involved and agreed to leave Switzerland for New York, Wertheimer turned the Chanel Perfume Showroom project over to the Chairman of the Board of Chanel America, Gregory Thomas. As was his custom, Wertheimer then walked away from the project with no intention of returning until it was completed. He should have had no reason to be concerned, as the project was seemingly in good hands. However, the creation of the new showroom was no sooner underway, when a dispute arose concerning the involvement of Tom Lee, the designer chosen by Gregory Thomas to work with Mademoiselle.

Tall and handsome in a tweedy sort of way, Tom Lee's creative background and record of achievement was outstanding. He was a prolific interior and industrial designer with a history of witty and imaginative displays and charming exhibits. A noted artist himself, Lee was au courant with the intricacies of the contemporary art scene. This inspired a close relationship with Coco, who had been heavily involved in the arts before her retirement. On the surface, Tom Lee was an inspired choice to work with Coco Chanel on the showroom. And that was a problem for Gregory Thomas. Tom Lee's background in the arts was a little too inspiring for Thomas, who had known Coco in France before the war and wanted to be her foremost contact in America. Unfortunately, Thomas did not have a background in the art world that Coco reveled in.

Her support for art and music had been unflagging, and most people she associated with in the pre-war era were of that background. The collapse of Czarist Russia left the Ballets Russes, and their impresario Sergi Diaghilev, without funds until Coco financed his production of the controversial *Rite of Spring*. Incidentally, she became in the process, lover of the composer, Igor Stravinsky. Among other projects, she designed costumes for the Ballet Russes' *The Blue Train*, while Picasso, an admirer of Coco, designed the backdrops.

The arts mattered to her and Tom Lee's connections there resonated. Without realizing it, Lee had committed the sin of cutting in on Gregory Thomas's relationship with Coco Chanel. Gregory Thomas resented this development and set about to reinstate primary status with Coco. He knew that Tom Lee, in spite of an international background, was not fluent in colloquial French. In what seemed to be an informal meeting of the three of them concerning the scope of the project, Gregory Thomas used his facility with language to embarrass Tom Lee.

Initially, Lee was able to keep up with Coco and Gregory Thomas in a conversation that began as a three-way dialogue in English and French. Eventually, while ostensibly including Tom Lee, the conversation lapsed into vernacular French. After the meeting went on for a while, Gregory Thomas turned to Lee and asked him in English if he agreed with what had been discussed.

Not wishing to confess that he had not understood much of what was said, Tom replied that he understood and concurred.

Too late, he discovered that he had agreed to be in charge of a much larger project than he had anticipated or budgeted for. Originally, he thought he would be involved only in the design and installation of the main showroom. Now he found that he was responsible for the design of the entire Chanel floor, and he had agreed to do this for the same financial package that he was to receive for the main showroom alone. This discussion of the change of responsibilities was probably not an accident or even unplanned. It was Gregory Thomas's way of deliberately putting Tom Lee down in front of Coco, and in the process, reducing costs for Chanel Perfumes.

Gregory Thomas's Machiavellian penchant for saving money was something that I would encounter as the work on the showroom progressed. For Tom Lee it would intensify the pressure to perform beyond realistic expectations.

CHAPTER 3

Me?
The Assistant to the World's
Most Famous Couturier?

Tom Lee was highly qualified for the showroom project, a prestigious assignment that he planned on handling alone. However, because of Gregory Thomas's maneuver, Lee had to make up for his increased time on the job and decreased compensation for time spent. This expansion of responsibilities had the potential to hurt a creative design business that required his attention on myriad levels, as well as take him away from other clients, many out of town. Since budgetary constraints precluded hiring an expert to fill in for him, Tom turned to me, in spite of my lack of qualifications.

In truth, the Chanel showroom project was an entirely new experience and one for which I was ill prepared. I was 31, had spent three and a half years in the army in World War II, married after graduation from Rhode Island School of Design, and had a young family to support. I did freelance work in sales promotion for several clients, created displays for Revlon Cosmetics, and painted a mural for the specialty store Bonwit Teller. But none of this paid very well.

Having studied advertising design at RISD, I decided to look for work in this field. When I heard that the noted designer Tom Lee was adding advertising to his many faceted creative involvements, I applied for a position with his company, Tom Lee, Ltd. To my surprise I was hired, but after several weeks without advertising assignments I became discouraged. When Tom Lee called me into his office one morning I expected a dismissal. Instead, he told me that he was in charge of the design and construction of a new showroom for Chanel Perfumes, and that I was to be involved on a day-by-day basis with the partly completed showroom, working as the assistant to the famous couturier, Mademoiselle Chanel.

A man usually displaying a calm demeanor, Lee seemed tense, a strained expression on his patrician features. As he discussed this project with me, there was an edge to his voice, as if the subject was somehow unpleasant. While this new development meant I still had a job, it could possibly be unpleasant for me, too. It was certainly an intimidating assignment; I knew of Mademoiselle, the famous Coco Chanel, but only that she had been a world class celebrity. I needed work but I lacked experience in showroom design or interior architecture, and had never worked with a celebrity. Furthermore, I spoke almost no French. On the surface it looked as if I had few qualifications for this work.

I had little time to contemplate this bewildering assignment. The day after informing me of my new job, Tom Lee took me to visit the future Chanel Perfume Showroom. The unfinished space occupied the seventh floor of a building on 58th Street at Fifth Avenue; the lower floors were occupied by a retail store, *The Tailored Woman*.

An elevator took us up to a small lobby on the Chanel floor. A double door on the other side of the lobby opened to a large room that was to be the reception area. As we entered this room I saw that construction was well under way, and Tom described, in some detail, the plans for its completion. To the left were several smaller rooms where Chanel salespeople would attend to important retail fragrance buyers. Tom pointed out the long wall on the other side of the reception room where valuable antique Coromandel screens were to be installed. Two doors would be cut into the wall of screens: one for the receptionist and the other would open to the corridor leading to the Chairman's office. I was impressed and eager to start, though I had trouble following his detailed description of the proposed installations. It was obviously an extraordinary project, but it was still far from finished.

While we were talking, the reception room door opened and a short, dark haired woman and a monumentally large man entered. She was immaculately dressed in a white suit trimmed with black edging, and a matching hat. Of imposing bearing, the man wore a charcoal gray, European-styled suit, obviously hand tailored to better disguise his bulk. Tom introduced me to them: Mademoiselle Chanel and the Chairman of Chanel America, Gregory Thomas.

Standing next to Lee and Thomas, both well over six feet tall, the petite Coco Chanel was in no way diminished. There was about her an aura, a radiation of force that compelled your attention. And I could not help but notice a faint wisp of an alluring fragrance. It was, of course, N°5; I later learned she wore the perfume every day of her life. In her classic Chanel suit, adorned with multiple ropes of pearls, she looked much younger than her seventy years. Her hair was cut in bangs, and large, dark-rimmed glasses partially concealed her face. I could not help but notice her eyes, alert and piercing, as she quietly acknowledged me before turning back to Thomas and Lee. After a short conversation with Tom Lee, Chanel and Gregory Thomas moved on. Brief as it was, this meeting was a foretaste of the fascinating experience to unfold.

CHAPTER 4

Strange Stories from the Old Office

My next step, after introductions to Mademoiselle Chanel and Gregory Thomas, was to meet personnel of the Chanel USA office. The old office, while only a few blocks away from the new showroom, was light years away in terms of concept. While impressive, with obviously expensive wood paneling, it lacked the flair and pizzazz one might expect from anything connected with the Chanel mystique.

On my first visit, I met with Gregory Thomas. He seemed quite friendly, and after we discussed my duties at the new showroom, he introduced me to members of the staff. I was relieved to find them cordial. After several sessions with Thomas, I used time between meetings to sort out the responsibilities of the staff. In addition to sales and distribution employees, several people functioned in unique capacities.

One man doubled as a kind of secret service and fraud protection officer. His job was to track down a shadowy organization that produced and sold bogus Chanel N°5. The way it usually worked: a glass bottle, close in appearance to the authentic perfume's vessel, was filled with whatever cheap perfume was available and sold to a gullible public at an enormous profit. Members of the criminal organization behind the phony fragrance frequented wharf areas in port cities, offering the fake Chanel as stolen cargo. The counterfeit N°5 was priced at about half of the true scent, but far above the actual cost of the substitute. It was a very profitable operation that succeeded because it played on the involvement of the buyer in an illegal transaction. Many people, oblivious to the difference between the cheap stuff and the real thing, went away happy. However, those familiar with Chanel N°5 found themselves stuck with dime store merchandise, but they could not complain to authorities since they had knowingly bought stolen goods. As the scam was seldom reported to the police, it was difficult to apprehend the criminals. One of the few leads the Chanel fraud protection people had to go on was the imitation bottle, so they concentrated on discovering the source of those. But as this was truly a fly-by-night operation, when one bottle factory was closed down by Chanel, another opened elsewhere.

It was all so intriguing: the image of Chanel security people in shadowy port areas, tracking down sinister types dressed like sailors or longshoremen who whispered in phony French accents to naive passersby about stolen merchandise. While the pursuit of the sellers of fake N°5 sounded like scenes from old black and white movies, the search for illegal glass factories conjured up versions of spy stories. Although the sale of phony perfumes began in the 1920s, the hunt for purveyors of bogus perfumes continued into the 1950s, and probably still today, as counterfeiting of prestige products is ongoing.

In addition to the fraud protection man, several other functionaries were friendly, talkative and often welcomed me into their coffee breaks. Knowledgeable about the behind the scenes activities of the Chanel Perfumes organization, they often chatted about what was *really* happening and kept me informed as events progressed.

Among the regulars at the Chanel office, seated at an empty desk in rather spacious quarters, a youngish man of unassuming demeanor always seemed pleased to have someone to talk to. He was, I found out, Jacques Wertheimer, the quiet and reserved son of the charismatic Pierre Wertheimer, but not heir to the business, and with no discernible function at Chanel Perfumes. As is often the case with sons of successful, dynamic men, he was a non-achiever. Coco referred to him rather scathingly as *The Kid*.

When I met him, he was on New York assignment—temporary duty, as every six months or so he would be shipped to another office, with nothing to do there either. From New York it might be Buenos Aires and then Singapore and so on.

I'll note here that I later learned his employment scenario continued until 1965 when his father died. Free from parental domination, Jacques retired to a quiet life, first in New York, and later in Switzerland.

CHAPTER 5

Chanel America's Renaissance Man:
Gregory Thomas

Fascinating details of Gregory Thomas's background emerged as time went on. While I admired Tom Lee for his creative strengths and ability to put the showroom together, he was not exactly amiable to me. Perhaps he resented me—a reminder of his problem with Gregory Thomas. Mademoiselle was an exacting but reasonable person, and proved to be a pleasure to work with. Thomas, a noted international lawyer, an officer of the French Legion of Honor and Chairman of Chanel America, turned out to be the most helpful. Although I did not realize it at the time, this was self-interest on Gregory Thomas's part, as his relationship with Lee had cooled considerably; he needed to rely on me to keep track of progress.

Imposing in appearance, Gregory Thomas stood a robust six foot eight, resembling a tall Winston Churchill, with a voice of Churchillian sonorousness. If anyone deserved to be called a "Renaissance Man," it was Thomas. Pleasant and affable on the surface, I soon realized he had a side, usually well hidden, of sharp steel—a side that, to his dismay, Tom Lee had discovered. The more I learned about Gregory Thomas the more I was in awe of him; fortunately he became a kind of mentor and was available for consultation on procedures and potential problems. He often dropped by the new showroom to give advice and encouragement, and several times took me to lunch at one of his favorites, Cafe Argenteuil. Conversations with the Chairman were not casual and I often felt he was testing me to discern how much I knew and what I was capable of. Eventually, perhaps because of these conversations, he inspired me to get involved in the creative process.

In Thomas's world of perfumes he reigned supreme. A consummate salesman, he was an oft quoted spokesman, not only for Chanel, but for the entire fragrance industry. But that was a mere slice of his wide-ranging accomplishments. In spite of his education in Switzerland and at Cambridge University, with doctorates from the Sorbonne and the University of Salamanca in Spain, he retained a common touch. He was so competent with idiomatic jargon and slang, during World War II, he was able to spirit a truckload of the essential oils needed to make perfume, and the formula for Chanel N°5, out of occupied France and on to America through neutral Spain. He did this by convincing border guards that his tank truck was loaded with non-essential agricultural chemicals. This dangerous and daring exploit took place just as Vichy, the puppet government of France, was taken over by the Nazis. At the same time, he rescued Pierre's son, Jacques, from occupied France. The rest of the Wertheimer family had escaped to America, and used the essential oils and formula for N°5 supplied by Gregory Thomas, to create an American company to make and sell Chanel perfumes throughout the free world.

A man of many talents and interests, Thomas owned a library of more than 8,000 books, including 19th century English poetry and 18th century illustrated books from France. He also collected rare stamps and early jazz records. Thomas loved to cook, belonged to several gourmet societies, was a member of the prestigious *Les Douze Gueles*, and was the only American to be elected to *La Club des Cent*, considered to be the most prominent gourmet society in the world.

Thomas's numerous attributes included his encyclopedic knowledge of wine. An eminent connoisseur with a cellar of over 100 bottles of the world's best vintages, he credited his robust health to the quality of the wines he drank on a regular basis. Thomas was considered such an expert extraordinaire that no one objected when he brought his own bottles to the finest restaurants in New York, "paying corkage, of course."

Perhaps the fine wines counteracted the ever present cigarettes, Gauloise, which he chain-smoked. When we often had occasion to talk, he spoke clearly, even with a cigarette dangling from the corner of his mouth. As he did not remove a cigarette except to use it to light up another, the ash would continually fall on his tie, making a smudge. His distinctive hand motion was to brush the ash off, which of course made the mark even worse. By the end of the day, his tie was a complete mess. So, on his way home he would stop at the Dollar Tie Store, purchase a new tie for the next day, and throw away the soiled one.

Thomas's imposing build and somewhat disheveled appearance contrasted sharply with Chanel, petite and always impeccably dressed, but they seemed to have considerable affinity. As Coco was also a chain-smoker, I often saw them smoking together and chatting away in what I assumed was their language of camaraderie: vernacular French.

CHAPTER 6

Tom Lee: Celebrated
American Designer

In contrast to Gregory Thomas, Tom Lee dressed in a style that showed a flair for fashion. He usually wore faultlessly cut, tailored suits or expensive looking sports jackets and slacks. When the occasion demanded he would take off his jacket, roll up his sleeves, and plunge in to make changes or additions to whichever project he was involved with. While I admired Tom Lee for this hands-on approach, and even more for his creative talent, he was not someone I felt comfortable with, or could go to with a problem. In the long run, while difficult to see how I could fit into his organization, I could not but be impressed with his accomplishments.

Like Gregory Thomas, Tom Lee had an extraordinary background. He was a noted painter as well as designer, with an international reputation. Born in Costa Rica, son of the American Consul, he spent his early years in Brazil, Portugal, and England. He studied art at the Traphagen School and the National Academy and taught at the Fashion Institute of Technology. Multitalented, he created sets and costumes for a number of musical comedies, including *Louisiana Purchase*, and backgrounds for the American Ballet Company. In World War II he was commissioned a lieutenant in the Eighth Air Force, and served overseas in the counter-intelligence branch of the Office of Strategic Services, retiring as a major.

As Display Director for Bonwit Teller and later Bergdorf Goodman, he was noted for his witty and imaginative window displays. Tom's display fantasies included the nostalgic "Torch Light Parade" for the Golden Jubilee celebration of the Fifth Avenue Association, the "Christmas Merry-Go-Round" at Lever House, exhibitions at the Metropolitan Museum, the Smithsonian, the Brussels World's Fair and the Moscow World's Fair.

One of the best known names in the design field, Tom Lee was an obvious choice to creatively plan and supervise the various rooms and fine art installations that were to make the Chanel Perfume Showroom unique. Beyond his creativity as a designer, Tom's ability to work effectively with Mademoiselle Chanel was an important consideration that insured the success of the project and indirectly contributed to her triumphant return to eminence in the world of couture.

In addition to his stint with Chanel, Pierre Wertheimer assigned Tom to work with two other companies he controlled: those of Elizabeth Arden and Helena Rubenstein. Tom designed their New York salons, showrooms, and product packaging, and I was also involved in these projects, although in a minor way. Mademoiselle Chanel and Madame Rubenstein got together at this time and enjoyed many hours of conversation. As they both rose from abject poverty to spectacular success in the same industry, I imagine if their discussions had been taped they would have provided material for several books.

CHAPTER 7

Working with a Genius

Before I began to work with Mademoiselle Chanel I knew very little about her, except that she was of another era, a famous person to be sure, but a kind of holdover from the past. Gradually it became apparent that Mademoiselle was still charismatic and a powerful presence, with absolute perfection in matters of taste. While not the raving beauty of her earlier years, Chanel at seventy was very attractive. Usually dressed in one or another of her famous suits, festooned with loops of pearls, and bedecked with distinctive jewelry, she was obviously someone of distinction. Composed and sure of herself, she exuded an inner dignity.

The aura of celebrity that surrounded Mademoiselle prompted me to move cautiously in my first contacts with her. Luckily, I did not know she was a reputed martinet and a most finicky perfectionist, so I was not inhibited by knowledge about problems that could arise when working with her. On the whole, our relations remained cordial. Having been warned of Tom Lee's problem due to his inability to fully comprehend vernacular French, I decided that with my limited language skills I would not risk a similar situation. For the entire time I worked on the project I did not even say "Bon jour" to anyone, especially Mademoiselle.

Fortunately, that was not a hindrance as she spoke English well enough. Her accent was charming, though her voice, due to a lifetime of smoking, was somewhat husky. Mademoiselle, like many celebrities and just about everyone else at that time, was rarely seen without a cigarette. In practically every photograph she is holding a cigarette or actually smoking. I do not think this was an affectation; it was a stimulus to creativity and integral to her way of life. While cigarette smoking has been proven to be the cause of serious health problems, the proven cognitive uptick from nicotine is now being studied by science.

After 13 years away from her great passion, creative work, her happiness at being back was often evident by her remarks and comments about our project as she went about her imaginative way. As she worked, she often talked on in French, in a kind of singsong voice, as if she was chatting with someone. It was incomprehensible to me, but that did not matter to either of us, as I came to realize this was a kind of conversation with herself. When she spoke to me in English, however, it was direct and to the point. I quickly learned to act on her suggestions immediately.

We did not have conversations per se, she would give me instructions and that was it. I think she considered me a person to give orders to, and was pleased that I could carry them out, but nothing beyond that. Her decisions were not discussible. There was never any chitchat or repartee of any kind. Mademoiselle treated me kindly and corrected my mistakes without rancor, but there was no familiarity permitted, and I did not ask for any. I knew my place and kept it. On the other hand, my relationship with the powerful, yet pragmatic, Chairman, Gregory Thomas, remained open and personal.

In the beginning, there was the question of how to address Coco Chanel. In France, when a woman reached 40, she automatically became "Madame," married or not. But Chanel, unmarried at 70 was still "Mademoiselle," and stayed Mademoiselle her entire life. Later, after her successful return to fame, when she had become a living legend, not just in France, but throughout the world, she was no longer just Mademoiselle, but La Grande Mademoiselle.

Her real name was Gabrielle, but she rarely used it. She was "Coco" to friends, and "Mademoiselle" to everyone else. Her aversion to her given name possibly came from her years in the orphanage. She was addressed as Gabrielle by the nuns when they criticized her, presumably often enough, as she was always a free spirit. I would not have dreamed of calling her Coco; I always addressed her as Mademoiselle.

CHAPTER 8

Chanel's Love of Mirrors, Beige, and Black and White

It was not long after my orientation at the old Chanel office that I started working in earnest on the new showroom. Initially my contributions were trivial, but by watching and listening, I saw how things worked, or didn't work, including the results of tensions between Tom Lee and Gregory Thomas. Usually when Tom Lee was there, Gregory Thomas was not. But if I was there without Lee, the Chairman often came by. Even when the Chairman did not put in an appearance, I often had the rather eerie feeling that he was hovering just around the corner or down the hall, and that little happened without him knowing about it. As the offices for the staff from Chanel USA began to be activated, I often saw friends I had made at the old office in the new showroom. We usually exchanged friendly greetings and I gave them progress reports as we went along. I am sure that much of this went back to their boss, the Chairman.

I also got to know the workmen employed by Tom Lee, Ltd. Many of them were refugees with special skills that involved metalwork, fine carpentry, cabinetmaking, laminating, various painting effects, and so on—techniques acquired by working in various European countries. As I would be working closely with them, I needed to know their capabilities. Because of their old country skills they were able to craft almost anything required for completion of the showroom. As I also worked for Tom Lee, they were personally supportive, often helping me resolve problems that arose beyond my capacities. I would guess that Tom kept in touch with my progress, even when he was away, as these workmen followed my activities closely.

The first project I actually worked on was the long corridor leading to Gregory Thomas's office. This was an area that would receive Coco Chanel's special imprint: her love of the splendor of mirrors. In her Paris showroom and in her unique apartment over the studio at 31 Rue Cambon, mirrors magnified the exotic ambiance. In keeping with this affinity, one side of the long corridor was a floor-to-ceiling wall of mirrors. For the other wall, Coco insisted on one of her favorite colors: beige. Her exact description of the shade she requested was, "the color of wrapping paper." This color effect was not obtained by painting the wall; instead, Tom had his craftsmen construct and install a series of panels covered with woven grass cloth from the Philippines. The natural beige of the grass cloth achieved the color she wanted. With these panels, slightly bowed out from within by fiberglass molded foam panels, Tom now had the softness desired as a contrast to the wall of glass. The mirrors reflecting the panels created a wavelike effect.

The floor of the corridor, set in hallway-wide black diamond shapes against a white background, used a favorite Chanel color combination: black and white. As this was an often used motif for Chanel packaging, I saw that using colors she liked was a way of bringing her personal signature into the showroom. Reflected in the long wall of mirrors, the beige paneling and diamond shaped squares gave an illusion of depth. Walking down this hallway to the elegance yet to be discovered in the office of the Chairman, one would experience the excitement of embarking on a special journey.

The whole project was a special journey for me. As I worked with Mademoiselle and Tom Lee on the corridor, I realized that my lack of experience was not the handicap I had feared. Courses taken as a student at Rhode Island School of Design proved to be of great help, particularly those taught by John Howard Benson. A sculptor and calligrapher, he was a distinguished artist noted for his skill in carving letters in stone. In addition, his classes in esthetics were memorable at the time and proved invaluable.

Likewise, I had been fascinated with the collections of the Museum of Art at Rhode Island School of Design, and engrossed in lectures given by its director, Alexander Dorner. Now, as I went about my work in the showroom, recollections of his creative concepts—such as the interaction of people and museum art, and other avant-garde museum concepts—were gratefully recalled.

CHAPTER 9

The Chairman's Office: Opulence to Rival Coco's Parisian Apartment

To continue Chanel's beige aura, the grass cloth panels lining one wall of the corridor flowed into the Chairman's office, covering all of the walls. The warm hues of antique Provincial and French Regency furniture, with their rosy blond leather seats, emphasized Chanel's love of beige. On the floor, soft shades of a rare Shivan-Khilim rug accentuated the golden glow.

Hanging paintings in the Chairman's office became my first involvement in the installation of showroom treasures: rare and valuable works from Pierre Wertheimer's private collection. Here I assisted Tom Lee, with Mademoiselle supervising. Six of the paintings were by celebrated primitive painter, Le Douanier Rousseau, including his famous Monkeys, a spectacular jungle scene. There were two portraits by Renoir: the Lady with Jabot, and the other, an interesting choice, called Portrait of Gabrielle. While not of Gabrielle Chanel, it was a remarkable portrait. At the time, I wondered who that Gabrielle was and what Mademoiselle thought of the title. Mademoiselle did not usually collect paintings, but she did own an early Renoir and Rousseau's Sleeping Gypsy. Lighting of paintings is a perplexing task as spotlights, usually directed from the ceiling, often spill out past the paintings, on to the frame and the wall. To overcome this, Tom had ceiling lights installed that used metal frames. We adjusted these devices to light the canvases, without spillover; when the spotlights were turned on, the paintings seemed to glow. If the regular lights were turned off and the ceiling spotlights left on, it appeared as if the paintings were illuminated from within. I think Renoir would have appreciated our way of lighting his art, given his passion for luminosity. Although stylistically very different, the Renoirs and Rousseaus worked well together, generating a pleasant sense of excitement. When completed, the office was meant to be an oasis of culture and power where Gregory Thomas could engender substantial orders of Chanel products from bedazzled female fragrance buyers.

A large Gregory Thomas-size sofa, intended to be beige, but not yet upholstered was our next project. Covering the couch was a challenge since Mademoiselle wanted suede, a naturally beige leather made from kid skin. While she liked the look and feel of suede, goats are rather small and their skins would have had to be pieced together to cover the sofa's large expanse. It was impossible to do this without seams showing and that was not a look she would accept. Finally we arrived at a solution: the use of reverse calfskin. Calfskin turned inside out not only gave a kid skin effect, but could cover large surfaces. The result was a massive sofa; it was soft, comfortable, beige, and looked as if it were covered in suede. Mademoiselle not only approved but she occasionally took time to stretch out, luxuriating in the sybaritic comfort the outsized sofa provided.

(Upon returning to France, Mademoiselle used this same reverse calfskin technique to cover a large couch that she added to her exotic studio apartment in Paris. It replaced an antique, but less comfortable, settee. The substantial size and soft cushions of the new sofa provided a respite from her intense schedule of work and social interaction. At that time, upholstering with reverse calfskin was a new technique in France, and her use of it was lauded by noted interior designer Harve Mille as an example of Chanel creativity.)

Another facet of the opulent decor of the showroom would be a collection of 15th century Benin bronzes from Africa; however, they had not yet been delivered. While waiting for the sculptures, I went to the Tom Lee Ltd. office on West 55th Street to catch up on other pending projects. Tom was away on one of his out-of-town assignments, but the office ran well in his absence. Tom Lee's business organization consisted of people of various talents: an office manager, expediters, artists, account people, draftspeople, and others involved in various projects under Tom's supervision. There was only so much time Tom Lee could spend on any one project, so he needed competent people to fill in for him.

Such was the very capable Tom Lee Ltd. draftsperson currently assigned to the Chanel Perfume Showroom. She had worked closely with Tom to lay out the offices and installations, including the men's and ladies rest rooms. With walls of shiny, black ceramic tile, these facilities would be posh indeed, but a problem was slowing things down. Our draftsperson, with some embarrassment, confessed that she had trouble visualizing the interior layout of the men's room for the blueprints, as she had never seen a urinal. After the Tom Lee office closed for the day, she was ushered into the men's room to see what one looked like —problem solved.

Without much going on at the showroom, I was looking forward to a fairly relaxing day at the office. I had just settled in my cubicle to work on plans for additional installations, when the phone rang. It was Gregory Thomas requesting that I come to his office, and of course I went post haste.

He welcomed me and then turned to some small sculptures lying on his office table. He studied them for a short time and then got down to basics.

"Know about these?" Gregory Thomas asked.

I got the feeling this was some kind of test, but fortunately I had an answer for him; I knew about them from my studies at the Rhode Island School of Design.

"Yes," I said. "These are Benin Bronzes."

The sculptures originated in the no-longer-existing African country of Great Benin. As early as the 14th century, servants of the Oba, or King of Great Benin, used the difficult-to-master *lost wax* method of casting bronze at a time when this technique was almost unknown in Europe. The skill of casting and the high quality of the art of Benin Bronzes caused them to be featured in exhibits at major art museums. Coco selected these sculptures for the showroom as they would have been right at home with the marble Aphrodite, the Coptic head, the Venetian blackamoors, and other exotic works of art in Mademoiselle's sumptuous apartment above her atelier in Paris.

Gregory Thomas quickly got to the point. "Well," he said, "they came in unmounted; can you do something with them?"

This was *my* first experience with the Chairman's penny-pinching ways, and I recognized this was a challenge I probably should accept, in spite of my inexperience in museum mounting. If I could do the job rather than have Tom Lee bring in an expensive outside expert, there would be no additional cost to Chanel. There was nothing in this for me, except for the creative challenge. With Tom Lee out of town, I thought, *perhaps I have nothing to lose.* I was, after all, taking on the assignment directly from Gregory Thomas. With some misgivings, I agreed to mount and install these priceless bronzes.

They were sent over to the new showroom where I sketched out my ideas, showing the sketches first to Mademoiselle and discussing with her how she wanted them installed. She sanctioned the designs and showed me where they were to go. Working with Tom Lee's craftsmen, the mountings were soon completed and installed. Due to the exemplary skills of the craftsmen, bases worthy of these unique African artifacts now existed in the Chanel Perfume Showroom.

After the Benin Bronzes were in place, Mademoiselle voiced her approval. But Tom Lee did not mention the designs or the installation, although he could not miss seeing them or hearing about them from his work crew. Gregory Thomas was impressed, probably with the money he had saved, and he took me to lunch at one of his favorite restaurants. After a few minutes of desultory conversation, he questioned me about my background and capabilities. I realized that he was probing for something, and this was not just another friendly get-together, but his agenda was not revealed

The decor for the Chairman's office was complete except for a minor detail: a telephone for Gregory Thomas's desk. Evidently a suitable telephone was left out of the plans and an undistinguished, black, American phone (all there was in those days), sat on this beautiful French Provincial desk. On my own, without consulting anyone, I wanted to use an elaborate antique style, French telephone, modified to fit current technology. Here my intuition failed me as Gregory Thomas dug in his heels. His experience with the pre-war, French telephone system was so bad, evidently a common experience, that he wanted nothing reminiscent of it. He ended up with the plain, black, American phone on his desk. But at least the phone worked and I don't think anyone noticed or objected to this anachronism, not even Mademoiselle.

CHAPTER 10

Coco and Tom Create
a Dramatic Entrance

An impressive entrance to the Chanel Perfume Show-room was vital. The elevator door opened to a small, nondescript vestibule. Across from the elevator, a double door, lit by a spotlight, opened to the reception room. Tom and Coco decided to make the entrance dramatic with a door handle, both elegant and allegorical. Mademoiselle was justly fond of the Chanel N°5 bottle; the serene, almost masculine, art deco design had been an outstanding, successful alternative to the onslaught of delicate feminine perfume bottles from other couturiers. Her solution for the door handle: the emerald cut bottle stopper from Chanel N°5, suitably enlarged.

The next challenge was to discover how to create a much larger yet faithful reproduction of the original glass stopper. We called in a noted art glass artist who recommended sand casting and explained the process. "It is done," he said, "by pouring liquid glass into a mold and allowing the glass to harden, a method dating back to the Roman days." That sounded good to us. The artist, burly, bearded and dressed in bib overalls, went back to his studio to prepare and complete the process, returning it to us in about a week for installation. The natural beauty of the glass combined with the distinctive shape of the enlarged N°5 stopper, came through as we hoped—beautiful and inviting. The Chanel N°5 bottle stopper handle would open the door to the wonders of the showroom, just as the stopper on a N°5 perfume bottle opened to the scent of Chanel elegance.

CHAPTER 11

The Reception Area:
Where are the Tables and Chairs?

Coco's enchanting and arresting vision prevailed for the showroom's reception area and adjacent smaller showrooms. She imbued the space with an elegant ambience that would invisibly nudge retail store buyers into the proper romantic mood and mind set. Exotic Coromandel screens, when delivered, would be spread along one long wall to lend scenic beauty to the room. Entering the showroom would be a mesmerizing experience as a reflected view of the screens would be seen in a facing mirrored wall.

Not just the decor but the furniture would be memorable. Special-ordered, imported showcases, in keeping with Coco's love of black and white, were delivered. They were constructed of black angle iron (strips of metal folded the long way) and fitted with bone white milk glass shelves. The showcases were brought into the reception area and arranged in groups to eventually display the latest Chanel products.

At this point a crisis erupted: while the showcases had arrived, coordinating tables and chairs planned for the reception area had not been delivered. Upon checking, it was discovered that this furniture was out of stock and would not be available for some time. It was a serious problem as we were unable to find furniture locally that would mesh stylistically with the imported display cases. It was a crisis, perhaps, but not for the Chairman; he simply solved it by asking me to create tables and chairs that would coordinate with the showcases ("Under the supervision of Mademoiselle, of course.")

This was a foray into a new design area and another challenge. However, I did not view it as a difficult assignment; I had Mademoiselle's counsel, the style of the showcases as a guide, and skilled craftsmen to turn my sketches into finished furniture. At Mademoiselle's suggestion, the same angle iron construction used in the imported showcases was employed for the new furniture. Following suit, the table tops would be white milk glass, as in the display case shelves. For the chairs, squared off white leather seats would complete the vaguely art deco look of the black angle iron construction. When paired in conversational groupings with the imported showcases, the new furniture worked well. I had passed another test, mostly due to Mademoiselle's guidance and the skill of Tom Lee's versatile craftsmen. They pitched in and constructed the furniture as if it was a routine request.

With the chairs, tables, and showcases in place, sophisticated settings were emerging. Because of Mademoiselle's constant supervision, the Chanel look was very much in evidence. When the showroom was completed, a two-page editorial on it, in the August 15, 1953 issue of the American *Vogue* magazine, spoke of Coco's contribution, saying, "Black and white, perhaps her best known *imprimatur*, appears in black iron tables with milk glass tops, white leather chairs, and black iron showcases."

CHAPTER 12

A Paint Problem— We Incur Mademoiselle's Wrath

U nder the overall supervision of Tom Lee and creative inspiration from Mademoiselle, the installation of art and antiques was making excellent progress. As one achievement quickly followed another, I gained a feeling that nothing was impossible; any design concept could be realized. Whatever Mademoiselle asked for, we accomplished. An energy about her radiated creativity, a kind of enchantment that made each day special—days that enabled me to reach inside myself for previously unknown qualities.

We moved along at full speed, but in a way, skating on thin ice. One day the ice developed serious cracks. A seemingly easy assignment, it should not have gone wrong. It involved painting one of the sales rooms a shade of red to match a color sample Mademoiselle had provided. It was a routine job; I was unaware of the importance of this particular shade of red, as were the painters, who worked up paint samples that she approved. The job seemed on track, and that night the walls were painted.

The next morning I knew I had a problem. For the first time during the showroom project, Mademoiselle was excited and angry. All I could fathom from her diatribe was that the color was absolutely wrong: "Too much brown!" This outburst communicated that the exact shade of red was vital. While new color samples were feverishly and carefully worked on, I checked around to uncover the real problem. It turned out that this particular color symbolized a political issue between Coco and Pierre Wertheimer. In 1946, while still feuding, she had threatened to go into competition with his biggest moneymaker, *Chanel N°5*, by bringing out a perfume called *Mademoiselle Chanel*. The color of the package for this new product was not the standard Chanel black and white, but a particular shade of magenta. This was the color we needed to match.

Threatened competition from Mademoiselle had been the last straw to convince Wertheimer to lure Coco back into the organization. Whether Coco, by bringing this color into a prominent place in the showroom, was reminding Wertheimer of that episode, remains a question. But she was specific about wanting the exact shade of her chosen color.

In spite of the new and approved sample, the second round of painting turned out as wrong as the first. Now Mademoiselle was really angry and showed it by her very vocal protests. As I had no answer to the problem, I feared our good working relationship was in danger. It did not help that I now knew why she was so unhappy as I did not have the slightest idea how to solve this strange puzzle.

Finally, one of the craftsmen, who had often been helpful, stepped in, explained what had gone wrong, and told me what to do about it. "It is not a paint problem," he said, "but a lighting problem." Unbeknownst to me, light from fluorescent tubes of that time turned reds a brownish shade. We quickly installed incandescent lighting and *Voila!* the problem was solved. Mademoiselle regained her composure, and our harmonious working relationship resumed.

CHAPTER 13

Coco Chanel's Unique Signature: Coromandel Screens

Most of the art and antiques had been installed, with the exception of the Coromandel screens—Oriental treasures that I was unfamiliar with, but knew to be reputed of great value. Not much was happening at the showroom, and Mademoiselle was there less frequently. Tom Lee was away again, and as there was little to do on my own I decided to find out about these mysterious Chinese screens. Before I began my search at the New York Public Library, I thought I should inform Gregory Thomas. He seemed interested in my quest and asked me to report on my investigations.

After I finished my research, Thomas discussed the importance of Coromandel screens to the New York showroom, over lunch. I learned they were a truly unique Coco Chanel signature, dominating her exotic apartment in Paris and often the background she was photographed against. To emphasize the Coco Chanel connection, Thomas said the screens would occupy a focal point in the reception room and needed to be installed in a way that would accentuate their innate beauty.

I felt the research and conversations with the Chairman

would prepare me to assist Tom Lee with the upcoming installation. I now appreciated the significance of the screens to the Chanel mystique and my studies on Coromandel (its origin and manufacture), provided an understanding of their construction. I learned the screens, originally from 16th century China, took years to complete, as creating them was a complex and painstaking procedure. It began with panels of soft wood, which were less subject to shrinkage or expansion than hard wood. These panels were coated with layers of clay, which when suitably dried were pumiced to a super smooth surface. Then came the lacquer, from the sap of Asian sumac. In liquid form the lacquer is toxic, but in 16th century China, people were evidently expendable, as about 30 layers of lacquer were applied to each side of the 24 panels. A darkened room, where water continually coursed, provided the humidity necessary to keep the lacquer flowing properly. The carefully brushed on coatings required months to dry, with painstaking sanding between each layer. After the 30 coats of lacquer, and sanding with increasingly fine abrasives, the surface was glossy black and rock hard.

Designs were cut into the panel and painted. Using gold and silver leaf, shark blood, or other exotic pigments, artisans achieved a jewel-like landscape or still life against the gleaming black of the lacquer. The visual effect of massed Coromandel screens was powerful and dramatic, as displayed in Mademoiselle's glamorous apartment in Paris. It was an anticipated, resplendent effect for the new showroom.

After several days of additional research I returned to the office, expecting several more days of relaxation before the appearance of Tom Lee. Soon after getting to the office, however, Gregory Thomas called, asking me to join him at the showroom. When I arrived, Mademoiselle was there, as well as the Chairman, and it was obvious why I had been summoned.

The Coromandel screens had arrived. The venerable antiques, unpacked and spread out, took up much of the reception area's floor space. Gregory Thomas and Mademoiselle were standing off to one side and I joined them. It was quickly apparent this was not a casual meeting. As though electrically charged, Gregory Thomas stood in a way that his great bulk seemed even more formidable.

He was succinct; his voice radiating authority, he said, "We are behind schedule and we need to catch up." He paused, then continued with an ominous declaration: "Tom Lee is out of town, but the Coromandel screens must be installed as soon as possible." He paused again, stared at me intensely, and said, "We want *you* to install them."

Dumbfounded by his pronouncement, I did not know how to answer, so I said nothing. In response to my silence, the Chairman softened his decree by adding that Mademoiselle agreed with this decision and would be there, whenever I needed help or advice. I was wary and worried, with good reason; this was an intimidating challenge. My lack of experience did not bode well for success as there were so many possibilities for failure. I had never been involved with anything as fragile or precious as these treasures, which were not only frightfully expensive, but irreplaceable. If damaged they could not be repaired. While I realized this was another example of Gregory Thomas saving money, this time was different. I had managed to achieve some small success on much less important projects, but if I failed on this one, the results would be catastrophic.

If I turned Gregory Thomas down I might be replaced, and I needed the work. While I lacked experience in this area, the fact that Mademoiselle would be there to back me up, made the whole preposterous thing possible. As I had little choice, I accepted the responsibility to take over the installation of the Coromandel screens. With my head spinning, I returned to the office as a kind of refuge while I considered how this monumental task could be accomplished. It was a daunting assignment; without Tom Lee, I was on my own. On the other hand, it was an affirmation of my capabilities from both the Chairman and most importantly, Mademoiselle.

My studies of the Chanel Coromandel screens intensified now that I saw them close up. The two magnificent twelve-panel screens sparkled with intricate designs. On each panel a different and beautiful pattern of incised and brilliantly colored landscapes and flowers ran from top to bottom. When assembled they would become a stunning panoramic visual. Too tall for the walls of the reception room, they would have to be cut to fit. The problem was how to trim the top of the screens without them appearing edited. The second step would be to size the screens to fill one wall of the reception room exactly. Two doors would be cut into the Coromandel and needed to be positioned over existing showroom doors. The cutting of the screens for the new doors could not leave conspicuous marks. When closed, it was to look like a solid wall of Coromandel. Not an easy task, it permitted no mistakes of any kind in cutting and installation. It had to be perfect the first time.

The next day as I studied the screens, still spread out on the floor, a messenger arrived with a package. At that time the New York City Post Office could not deliver documents and parcels without a delay of several days. Since expedient delivery and transport of packages and other communications were of utmost importance to businesses, private messenger services were created. The messengers, mostly older men of scruffy appearance, were old-time New Yorkers who knew their way around the city by subway and bus. In spite of age and various handicaps they made their rounds in fairly short order.

This messenger was a real schlump: bent over, gangling, with thick glasses and a staggering gait. Seeing people across the room, and interested only in delivering his package, he made a beeline toward us, walking—clump, clump, clump—right across the Coromandel screens. No one dared to yell at him or try to get him off the screens for fear he might panic, run or fall, or do anything that could damage them. Delivery received, he was quickly and firmly escorted to the door on a path away from the screens. Luckily, the tough old Coromandel survived without a scratch, but it was a nervous few minutes for everyone witnessing this potential catastrophe. And thankfully, neither Mademoiselle or the Chairman were in the showroom while this was happening, although I am sure they heard about it from the Chanel staff who were.

Starting the Coromandel project, I needed all the help I could get from Mademoiselle. Fortunately, she was present almost every day during the installation, and I could turn to her for advice, reinforcement of my decisions, and discussions about the progress of the work. My conversations with Mademoiselle were always formal, never in any way familiar. Although she was usually in a good humor, there were boundaries I did not venture past. Mademoiselle's penchant for interior monologues continued, interrupted occasionally by comments addressed to me, significant and increasingly helpful.

The first steps were to set a time table and get cost estimates on cutting, piecing, and installing the panels. From the head of the Tom Lee work crew, I learned the names of four experienced cabinet makers. They came in, examined the screens, and after careful consideration returned with estimates in general agreement: all quite high, which I expected. However, after conversations about their method of working, I felt dissatisfied with the idea of using modern tools on delicate works of art.

Having been in Japan as a member of the American Army of Occupation, I had seen Japanese craftsmen work and the tools they used, and I felt that traditional Asian methods should be considered. I discussed this with Mademoiselle and she agreed. I then telephoned the Asian Art curator of the Metropolitan Museum of Art and asked if he could provide the name of an art restorer, particularly one highly skilled with antique lacquer.

"Yes," he said. "The restorer is Japanese and a real craftsman who has much experience working with lacquer. But what would he be expected to do?"

"Cut and piece Coromandel screens," I told him.

I heard him gasp over the phone, and it was obvious he was about to say *no way*. But when I explained that Mademoiselle Chanel was the artistic director of the project, he reluctantly agreed to send down the Metropolitan Museum's expert.

The restorer, short, sturdy, and seemingly knowledgeable, examined the blueprints showing where the screens were to be installed and the cuts needed for the doorways. He measured the room, including the ceiling height and a few days later gave me his estimate. It was so far below that of the others I called him and told him that he had the lowest estimate, but it was too low, and he should raise it. He added a substantial amount, but his estimate was still way below the competition. Naturally he got the job, but I am not sure he broke even, as the work turned out to be much more complex than he imagined.

To begin the Coromandel installation, the restorer brought several helpers, also Japanese, who I presumed were skillful artisans with experience in the use of traditional tools. As I have mentioned, the screens were too tall for the room, and the first task was to cut about a foot off the top, without the screens looking incomplete. This, I thought, would call for skills of the Far East; but when the restorer's team commenced cutting the screens, I was aghast and completely at a loss. They started the work using a modern, power driven, circular saw. This was in complete opposition to my reason for selecting the museum restorer in the first place, and in my opinion, absolutely wrong. And indeed it was the wrong approach, as the rock-hard lacquer burned out the motor of the circular saw in short order. Mademoiselle and I talked with the restorer, reminding him that the Coromandel screens, precious items from the Orient, should be treated with respect and suitable tools should be used.

At our request, returning to his roots, the restorer had his assistants use traditional Japanese hand saws. Shaped the opposite of American saws, they are narrower at the handle and wider at the other end. Instead of pushing down using force, you pull up toward you, gently. The blade of thin steel is high quality and extremely sharp. Validating my instincts, the job now proceeded successfully!

When the craftsmen finished, there stood the solid wall of Coromandel, without any sign of cutting and fitting. The two doors were not apparent when closed. When the first door opened, the receptionist would be seen in her office, ready to give assistance. The door to the corridor leading to the Chairman's office would be opened only for a select few.

Everyone was pleased the installation had worked out so well. On leaving, the restorer bowed several times; we shook hands and he and his crew departed. Relieved and happy with the triumphant completion of this difficult project, I called Gregory Thomas's office. He was away, and Mademoiselle, usually on hand, was not available either. The fact that these two important people were not present at this auspicious moment bothered me, but it quickly turned out that their absence saved me from being exposed as a complete bungler.

With the screens in place, everything looked the way it should, until I tried to open the doors, cut into what was now a wall of Coromandel. To my complete surprise and horror, neither door would open. Unfortunately, when the Coromandel was cut and applied to the existent doors, the added thickness did not allow the hinges from the old doors to open. I was stunned and in despair by this revelation of technical failure. My inexperience, it seemed, had caused a monumental and possibly unsolvable error.

By good luck, I was saved again by my friends from the regular work crew. They came up with the answer: offset hinges that swung wide, allowing the doors to open and close with ease. It was a simple solution by professional craftsmen that I could never have figured out. I am not sure if either the Chairman or Mademoiselle were aware of the potential disaster. When they finally saw the completed Coromandel installation, the doors worked well and everything was beautiful. Both seemed pleased with the final result: Mademoiselle with the esthetics and the Chairman with the financial advantage gained from not paying an outside expert to oversee the project. I felt deeply appreciative that this highly visible undertaking, with its accompanying stress and near catastrophes, had proven successful.

CHAPTER 14

Vogue and Hollywood
are Particularly Impressed

During the course of the showroom construction, I witnessed a change in the attitude of Mademoiselle. When I first began to work with her, she appeared reserved, and at times detached; as the project proceeded, she became actively involved in a personal way, supervising every detail. It was as if, through the process of on-going creativity, the Chanel drive resurfaced with its old intensity. Radiating vitality and enthusiasm, she was obviously primed for greater involvement in her passion: creative work.

As a result of her thirteen-year hiatus from the fashion world, the formerly famous Coco Chanel was new to the American media. Rediscovered by reporters, her command of the English language allowed them to feature her in numerous press conferences. Her acerbic wit and repartee endeared her to many who covered her activities. Not limited to fashion publications, the popular press also ardently reported her lively comments and vibrant life style.

Even with her heavy schedule at the showroom, Mademoiselle spent time with admirers. In addition to the media this included significant retailers and new friends—stimulating people from the New York fashion world. Her many social engagements, as well as her creative approach to the Chanel Perfume Showroom, resulted in resurgent celebrity, at least in America. As Pierre Wertheimer had planned, important people were intrigued and came to visit the showroom. Most had not been privy to Chanel's opulent surroundings in Paris. Although she slept in a simple room at the Ritz, her magnificent haven above the shop at Rue Cambon, was where she met with cultural leaders of the world. This had been an oasis of serene, unequivocal taste, seen only by a privileged few. Now Americans had something similar to view for themselves: Coco's fabulous artistry in New York.

Vogue was particularly impressed. A two-page editorial in the August 15, 1953 edition, featured photos of the showroom just after completion. It included views of her trademark Coromandel screens, showing the doors both opened and closed, and a glimpse of the mirrored corridor. On the opposite page, below the photo of Gregory Thomas's office, the copy read, *"Mlle Chanel, Famous Clothes Designer, Puts Her Special Imprint on These Rooms."* They did not say *former* clothes designer; they said *famous* clothes designer. The copy on the facing page went into enthusiastic detail about Coco Chanel's creative contribution to the new headquarters of Chanel Perfumes. *Vogue* said, *"Here too, is the unmistakable imprint of Chanel herself— a small dynamo of a woman, incisive, nervous, ineluctably French, possessed of accurate taste as some people are of perfect pitch."* *Vogue* also noted that, *"...she supervised every detail of the decor."*

It was obvious to the American media that Coco Chanel was a dynamic force in the world of high fashion, a personality to be reckoned with; and most valued by the press, she made good copy. Coco's social life was once again exciting; she made news wherever she went.

While I knew from working with her she was incredibly creative, the media attention revealed that Mademoiselle was much more; she was, by all accounts, an astounding talent in many venues. At the time, trade publications, particularly *Woman's Wear Daily*, edited by fashion authority John Fairchild, kept me informed. *The New York Times* and other assorted consumer publications following Mademoiselle's career, helped keep the details alive. The reports escalated rapidly, stories of her life and career morphed into an almost ceaseless barrage of information—and misinformation.

To glean the facts of Coco Chanel's background, I studied her past and discovered evidence of America's appreciation for her. In 1931, movie mogul, Sam Goldwyn, offered to pay her a million dollars to invest his stars with her particular magic. He proposed that Coco visit the Goldwyn Studios in Hollywood to improve the fashion awareness of MGM actresses. In the depths of the depression, a million dollars *was a lot of money,* even for the prosperous Coco Chanel. Turning movie queens into fashion icons was a short-lived endeavor: the very individualistic stars of the cinema did not like to be told what to wear. It was, however, a publicity coup for both MGM and Chanel. For Goldwyn, photos of MGM actresses wearing Chanel garments were featured in newspapers and magazines. To Chanel's benefit, her brief visit to America was not only extremely lucrative, but of greater value, it introduced her to the American media.

They were so impressed, that even at that time, she was considered a celebrity. This reservoir of good will turned out to be of significant importance in post-war years.

In 1947, the war over, but still in exile, Coco remained obsessed with hatred for the original Chanel perfume agreement. With little else to involve herself, she made another attempt to obtain a legal judgment against Pierre Wertheimer. Her long time lawyer, Count Rene de Chambrun, who resided in New York, did not wish to return to France. He was married to the daughter of Pierre Laval, the discredited tool of the Nazis when they occupied France. Coco decided if Chambrun could not go to her, she would go to him. As usual, her legal efforts did not succeed, but her visit resulted in another productive meeting with the American press.

On her way from Switzerland to her embarkation at Cherbourg, she had been completely ignored by the European media. When the ship arrived in New York, a large group of reporters waited on the dock; Coco assumed they were there for Al Brown, a well-known American boxer on board. Because his comeback was sponsored by her friend, Jean Cocteau, Coco did not wish to upstage Brown, and she lingered in her stateroom. It took a while for the ship's captain to convince her that the reporters were there to interview her and her alone.

Coco, pleased to have a responsive audience, delighted them with quick and witty responses to their questions. One was: "What do you think of Dior's New Look?" This concept of dress design by a new name in couture, Christian Dior, had been exceedingly popular. Coco hated it and did not hold back her opinion of Dior and his so-called "new look." This creation, with its swooping fullness of fabric held in place by boning, was, Coco said, "the same cumbersome and uncomfortable 'old look' that I banished years ago." Coco made pithy remarks about the decline of the fashion industry and its cause: "men creating clothing for women." The American press loved it. While the European press ignored her comments, it was not long before these personal contacts with the American press assumed great importance for Coco. Their favorable reporting was instrumental in ensuring her successful return to eminence in the world of haute couture.

CHAPTER 15

"Dior Didn't Dress Women, He Upholstered Them!"

Through new friends in the fashion world, Coco once again became acquainted with the vagaries of contemporary haute couture, and she did not like what was going on. Since the end of World War II, fashion had moved decisively away from her ideal of comfort and fit. It was shifting back to a past she detested, back to girdles, corsets and boning, taking place in an industry dominated by males.

In 1939 when she closed down Chanel Industries, female designers were the mainstay of couture in France. These included *Vionnet, Lanvin, Alix, Louise Boulanger, Nina Ricci, the Callot sisters;* even her rival, *"that Italian,"* as Mademoiselle called *Schiaparelli.* But, no mater how talented, before *Chanel,* they were just *dressmakers,* as the title *couturier* was only applied to male designers. Now male designers dominated. Among them *Pierre Cardin, Piguit, Balenciaga, Fath, Balmain, Courreges,* and the one she disliked most, *Christian Dior.* Chanel looked askance at the ascendancy of men in the world of fashion. She felt couture was women's work, and was at her most vitriolic when describing male designers: "Men who did not create a garment by building it on a live model (as she did)." "They were," she quipped, "mere sketchers." Coco never worked from sketches, and derided those who did.

Her garments were created, bit by bit, piece by piece, on a tailor's dummy, albeit a live one. A long suffering young woman would stand practically motionless, in spite of occasional pin pricks and scissor jabs, while the garment was created on the spot, on her body. At the end of the ordeal, the model was usually exhausted, but not the indefatigable Mademoiselle who went on to her next creation.

Since the end of World War II, the new world of couture dictated by men altered everything. During the war, because of the huge amounts of textiles needed for uniforms, parachutes and other military necessities, fabric for civilian use was in short supply. The shortage continued even after the war was over. Women's apparel was limited by restricted fabric lengths that only allowed for short, tight skirts. During that time, fashion barely existed, even in France. With the war's end the wish for something fresh and exciting was in the air, but Coco Chanel was not part of this. Still tucked away in Switzerland, she missed out on dramatic changes taking place.

Christian Dior transformed the desire for change into reality. A relative newcomer to haute couture, but backed by textile magnate, Marcel Boussac, Dior threw out the restrictions on fabric and created *The New Look*. Skirt lengths dropped to mid-calf, were full and swirling, and supported by several layers of stiff petticoats, heavily starched. Boning and cinching changed the way garments fit and the way women looked. Gone forever was the skimpy look of the war years. Women luxuriated in the change. "The New Look" was an overnight sensation. Even fashion shows for Dior's line were different. Instead of the usual sedate parade of mannequins, beautiful models gyrated down the runway as if in a dance. Twirling and spinning, they paraded this new fashion, showing handbags, scarves and other accessories, as they swept along.

Dior was not alone in bringing out novel—even bizarre—looks. The current couturiers, mostly male, went way out with extremely exaggerated shapes. There was an outpouring of eccentricity in fashion, little of which the average woman could wear with any degree of comfort. Comfort was not a concern of male designers who gained freedom of expression by working from creative sketches. Unfortunately, this license did not always result in wearable clothes. In general, there was confusion about where fashion was heading as it mutated radically, and often, from season to season.

The new looks had only one naysayer: Coco Chanel. One of Chanel's maxims was "Fashion does not exist unless it goes down to the streets: the fashion that remains in the salons has no more significance than outfits designed for a costume ball." Many years ago, Chanel had freed women from artificial cinching and boning. Now men were returning the female figure to the prison of uncomfortable and physically limiting apparel. "Dior," Coco stormed, "did not dress women, he upholstered them!" She had never been concerned with "fashion"; it was, Coco felt, "a butterfly that flits away. Style," she said, "is constant. Like good taste, style is always in fashion." The new looks were transient, and in her opinion, the worst kind of fashion. Male designer domination was all that was needed to fire up Coco's passion for her kind of couture—to the point where there was no turning back. Particularly since Carmel Snow, editor of *Harper's Bazaar*, assured Coco that high-end, American ready-to-wear manufacturers would be delighted to be part of a Chanel Couture revival.

CHAPTER 16

Coco and Tom Design
an Elegant Outdoor Surprise

Although the showroom embodying Coco Chanel's creative flair was technically finished, an aspect of medi-
ocrity needed to be remedied. The view from the Chairman's office offered a dull, gloomy outlook: the blank brick walls
of nearby buildings. To provide an alternative view, a lively ur-
ban revitalization, in keeping with the distinctive surroundings
of the Chairman's office, was created. Working together, Coco
and Tom Lee designed an elegant outdoor surprise: a charming
little roof garden.

We built outer garden walls with white bricks, set back to
create space for greenery, raised flower beds, and flowering
plants. A white fiberglass awning provided shelter from the
elements, and along with the white walls, complete privacy. A
couch, covered with green waterproof material was set against
one wall. To provide a touch of elegance, a typical Chanel trea-
sure, a white marble ram from ancient Sumer, stood on a pedes-
tal near the green couch. Back in Paris, another Sumerian sculp-
ture (a lion), graced the mantle of her magnificent quarters over
the Chanel salon on the Rue Cambon. White metal chairs strung
with tightly woven white string accompanied the table; and the

floor, covered with green indoor/outdoor weather-proof carpet, emphasized the white of a marble-topped table. The total effect was an appealing oasis of green and white. It extended the impact of Coco's creativity and drew the eye of the viewer from the opulence of the Chairman's office to a pleasant natural world.

With the completion of the roof garden, we were in the process of wrapping things up for the project when Gregory Thomas, accompanied by Mademoiselle, came by for a last minute inspection. They seemed to be delighted that all had worked out so well. The Chairman thanked me for my part in the installation as did Mademoiselle and they left.

That was it, "goodbye" as far as I was concerned. Tom Lee no longer needed my services, and I was off to other experiences. It had been a roller coaster ride, not without its downsides, but all in all, an unforgettable experience that remains engraved in my memory.

CHAPTER 17

Hopes for a Sizzling Return
are Extinguished

With the showroom completed it was apparent that Coco Chanel was not about to rest on her laurels. Fueled by pleasure from again working creatively and upset about the domination of the fashion world by men, her creative fires, banked for so long, burst into flames. Determined to return to her great love, haute couture, Coco at 71, was ready to go back to work. Pierre Wertheimer, somewhat reluctantly, agreed to provide funds for her new venture. So, in 1953, financing in place, she returned to France and began the arduous task of putting together a new Chanel Couture Collection. In a renewal of her past, Coco moved back into her favorite apartment in the Hotel Ritz, close to her reopened headquarters at 31 Rue Cambon.

Although I no longer had personal involvement, the American press, consumer and trade, kept me abreast of the amazing news of the return of Mademoiselle to Paris. In addition, I was able to follow events as they happened through friends at Chanel who kept me informed of the twists and turns of the drama as it played out.

In Paris, news of the return of the almost forgotten Coco Chanel soon spread, but with lackluster enthusiasm. Thirteen years had gone by since she showed her last collection, and much had changed in the fashion world. Many thought this comeback attempt of a controversial, elderly, and probably out-of-touch designer, a major mistake. There was, however, considerable curiosity about what she was up to. Would the Chanel "New Look" be space-age Courreges, with mini-skirted models in strange fabrics and vivid colors? Would the hemline be up or down? Or would it be 'Atomic' Chanel, using the 'Old Chanel' as a launching pad for an entirely new concept? Expectations and emotions grew as Mademoiselle, trusty scissors dangling from her neck like a religious medallion, cut, snipped and pinned to complete her line. Fingers swollen with arthritis, she toiled on for hours that exhausted younger Chanel employees.

At the time of Chanel Couture's reopening, Coco's contributions to fashion and the lives of women in general, were history. Before going into retirement, Coco Chanel had left behind a life of fabulous achievement, breaking through, not just a glass ceiling, but a cast-iron one. In pre-war France, a woman single-handedly creating and running a large and profitable business, was not only unheard of, but unthinkable. It is not surprising that Chanel's success was resented by many.

In spite of the hostility of some, Mademoiselle's incredible impact on the lives of women lived on. Freeing women from uncomfortable, restrictive clothing, she produced instead, garments of timeless style and ultimate comfort. She had popularized healthy tans at a time when everyone above the rank of peasant kept their skin color an unhealthy white; introduced short skirts and bobbed hair; invented costume jewelry; and created the best-selling and most famous perfume of all, Chanel N°5. Primarily, at a time when women's rights barely existed, she showed by her own life example, that women had the potential to be free and independent. Yet, in spite of what she had accomplished, her achievements were practically forgotten or unknown to the current generation in 1953, even in France.

Before her return, her often acerbic comments had antagonized many, and now her bitter comments spewed forth again. Rants against the male-dominated fashion establishment, and male couturiers in particular, were daily tirades. To add to Coco's unpopularity, scrutiny of her wartime affair with German diplomat, Baron Von Dincklage, mostly overlooked, was revived, leaving a bitter taste for some.

But the problem went deeper. Particularly upsetting to the fashion industry and those in government, was Chanel's way of running her business and her life without regard to convention. To make matters worse, she created the giant enterprise of Chanel Couture almost entirely on her own, in the process becoming the richest self-made woman in the world. Coco was probably the first woman in France to successfully scorn tradition and achieve success of this kind. This was neither liked nor admired by those in France accustomed to men being completely in charge.

While this negative attitude towards women took place in the 20th century, it was not the first time a female challenged authorities. In the 18th century, during the French Revolution, a brilliant young woman, Marie Olympe de Gouges attempted to include rights for women in the new constitution. Her attempts at reform did not get far—in fact, quite the contrary. Not only did women's rights not become part of the French Constitution, she was punished for her effort and sentenced to execution by the guillotine. Code Napoleon was of little help. Personally, Napoleon was against educating women. He said, "I do not think we need to bother about the education of young girls; they cannot be better brought up than by their mothers. Marriage is their only destination."

Even in modern times women's rights in France were limited. They did not win the right to vote until the end of World War II, a mere few years before Coco's return. Things had not changed by 1953; the anti-female viewpoint of the establishment made it obvious that Chanel's independent way of life would create enemies. Her constant outspoken comments and challenges created more. At the time of the reopening of Chanel Couture, the mood of the public and press was not conducive to a happy reception. For those she had disparaged it was payback time. Even without seeing her new line, it was as if the entire fashion world was ready to march on 31 Rue Cambon and tear it down.

Mademoiselle selected the fifth of February, 1954, for her opening, as the number five had always been lucky, demonstrated by the incredible success of Chanel N°5. That February day, luck deserted her; the quietly elegant showing for the international fashion press and to fashion industry notables, turned out to be a disaster. The audience expected a show of exotic fashion like that of the current couture designers; instead, she offered classic Chanel style. In her youth Coco Chanel was a true revolutionary, but as it often happens, the youthful rebel had become a conservative. When revealed, the new Chanel line had nothing atomic about it. In fact, quite the opposite: on display was a revival of Chanel's pre-war offerings, more or less a continuing of her successful 1938 fashion message.

That evening at Rue Cambon, the Chanel Couture showroom looked as it did in the old days, even the iconic mirrored staircase, rebuilt, appeared as it was before the war. The classic Chanel look and fit, in quiet good taste, was the main fashion statement. Unlike the prancing and posturing of the Dior models, those of Chanel walked sedately down the stairs and on to the runway. There was no music, no theater, no excitement. At the presentation of the 130 creations, applause was scarce, the silence deep. Failure hung in the air.

Mademoiselle did not appear. As usual, she sat high up on the stairs, hidden from view, watching the proceedings from the many mirrors that allowed her to see, but not be seen. It must not have been an uplifting experience. Audience reaction was visibly negative; it was as if the entire fashion world had been waiting to get her and now it seemed they had.

For those who disliked her it was a time for vindicated celebration. The reviews were devastating. They said that, at 72, she was too old, and had been out of circulation so long she had no understanding of the contemporary world. According to, not only the French fashion press, but to the European media in general, her work was of the past and should have been left there. Even the normally friendly English press was just as unkind. The *Daily Express,* for example, called it "A Fiasco." It was "A Flop," said the *London Daily Mail.* The consensus of the critics was for Chanel to go back into retirement. They all agreed it was the end of the fashion career for this disagreeable, old woman. And so it seemed. Coco Chanel was, to all appearances, completely unwanted, with nowhere to go but away. For Wertheimer it was tragic. All the money spent and the hope for new business for Chanel Perfumes, based on the comeback of Chanel Couture was down the drain. Members of Wertheimer's board suggested that he cease financing the couture line, but he stood firm and promised continued support. But for what? It was apparent that the long awaited comeback was over before it even started.

CHAPTER 18

The Incredible Return of Coco Chanel

As it happened, Wertheimer had no need to worry. Her return had just begun: like the phoenix, Coco Chanel arose from the ashes. A few days after the debacle, Pierre Wertheimer paid a call on Mademoiselle. It was a revelation. If he expected a dejected, defeated person, who had given up any thought of continuing her career in couture, he found instead, a confident Coco hard at work on her next collection. Unbeknownst to Wertheimer, Mademoiselle was in the process of being saved by friends she had made in America. Representatives of American *Vogue* magazine, present at her Paris showing, liked what they saw and recommended that the collection be brought to New York. The expense of sending this huge collection to America, approved and paid for by Pierre Wertheimer, sent Coco Chanel on her way to an incredible reversal of fortune.

In New York, surrounded by friends and admirers, the collection, so disliked in Europe, was a smashing success—albeit a pared down showing, without music or frills. The publicity was glorious; retailers rushed to buy, and arrangements with a reputable ready-to-wear manufacturer were achieved. At least in America, Chanel was famous again for her couture. It took a little longer in France.

In America, to those she worked with, and particularly the

press, she was the charming, cheerful Mademoiselle, the one I knew, not the grim, lonely figure portrayed in Europe. Her friends in the media went all out: *Newsweek* was filled with praise and the great powerhouse of that time, *Life Magazine*, said, "She is influencing everything; at 72 she is bringing in more than a style—a revolution." *McCall's* called her, "The World's Most Elegant Woman." Both Diana Vreeland at *Vogue* and Carmel Snow at *Harper's Bazaar* were favorably impressed. Everyone had something good to say and everywhere kudos abounded. At its meeting in New York, America's most influential fashion authority, the Fashion Group, featured Chanel outfits; Neiman Marcus and other high end retailers quickly bought into the Chanel tour de force.

Back in Paris, for subsequent and now triumphal and influential showings, Coco's maxims on fashion, once ridiculed were again quoted and her clothing style lovingly endorsed. In a short time Chanel was again the most important couturier in France, and her clothes, in great demand, sold to the likes of Grace Kelly, Marlene Dietrich, Jeanne Moreau, and other celebrated people. Iconic French *Vogue* led the media revision by putting one of Mademoiselle's garments on the cover. Other European publications followed and plaudits came fast and furious. In a short time she was again referred to as "La Grande Mademoiselle." For Pierre Wertheimer, the horse lover, it was like winning the Derby at Epsom Downs. He happily bought out Chanel Couture, paying for all expenses connected with it, thus insuring the dominance of Chanel Inc., and leaving Mademoiselle free to create classic clothing.

Her competition, the despised male sketchers, gave up their bizarre creations, at least for a while. Gone were extravagant fashions that could be made from sketches but were never really wearable. Even Dior got in on the act, going back to Chanel's early styles to create a new line of relaxed, softly-fitted apparel, quite unlike his previous crimped and boned garments, so constructed they could stand up alone. These retro fashions were well received and French fashion was of the new world. A new world that was Coco's old world: youthful fashion silhouettes that guaranteed not only style that never faded, but wearable comfort and freedom to move.

It was an almost unbelievable comeback. F. Scott Fitzgerald maintained that there are no second acts in American life, but the second act of Chanel's life began in America. The first was gained in France by enormous talent combined with unstoppable drive. The second act could only have taken place in America. Without the assistance of friends made while she was the Creative Director of the Chanel Perfume Showroom in New York, Coco Chanel would probably have remained a footnote in fashion history.

CHAPTER 19

Coco, the Musical — Tragedy or Travesty?

I n 1962, amidst the euphoria of Mademoiselle's incredible return to fame, Broadway producer, Fredrick Brisson, applied for permission from Coco to do a play based on her life. He got nowhere with his proposal until Coco heard that Pierre Wertheimer had forbidden a Chanel play of any kind. That made Coco determined to go along with the idea, particularly when she heard *Hepburn* would play the part of Coco. That made sense to Mademoiselle as she thought the Hepburn proposed was *Audrey*. That would have been a good choice; the beautiful Audrey Hepburn looked much like the young Coco, and had the same slight build.

On the contrary, it was the tall, rangy, old-money aristocrat, 60-year-old Katherine Hepburn, Brisson had in mind. *Coco* was conceived as a musical, but as Katherine Hepburn was not known for her ability to sing or dance, this was a rather strange choice.

In spite of Coco's approval, it took several years to work out production details. The experienced team of Andre Previn for the score and Alan Jay Lerner for the lyrics, promised a musical triumph as Lerner's songs for *My Fair Lady* had broken records in the play and film. The film starred Audrey Hepburn, wearing clothes by Cecil Beaton. When Coco found out that the clothes for *Coco* were also to be designed by Beaton, she was indignant. And rightly so—the costumes for *Coco* were even worse than the ones for *My Fair Lady*. Although he deserved no kudos for the costumes, Beaton didn't care much for the rest of the production. He thought the book was lousy and Previn's score banal. The audience didn't care; they had Hepburn.

Originally *Coco* was to be about Mademoiselle's early days, but to make it into a Hepburn vehicle, it was altered to spotlight Coco's later life. That resonated somewhat true to life, as Hepburn, like Coco, was noted for her independence. In the play, Hepburn, as Coco, having discarded several lovers along the way, climbs the stairs to success. In the end, she finds herself at the top, alone and lonely (which is actually what happened). When the final script was outlined to Coco, she commented that rather than a musical *comedy*, it seemed more a tragedy. In spite of poor critical reception, it was a triumph for Hepburn, a star attraction who won the hearts of the audience with her performance—not exactly Coco, but first rate Katherine Hepburn.

To me it was a travesty; I saw the play with friends. They liked Hepburn and they liked the play. I, on the other hand, had expected to see at least some resemblance to Mademoiselle and her life on stage that evening. That I didn't was not unusual as most of the Hepburn movies were about Hepburn being Hepburn. The sold out audiences for *Coco*, applauded that, but the movie rights, acquired by Paramount, were never put into production. After Hepburn went on to other engagements, a French star, Danielle Darrieux, took over. Without Hepburn, *Coco* sank without a trace. Although invited to the premiere, Mademoiselle, at 86 and increasingly feeble, never saw the production, supposedly her life story. My guess is that she probably did not want to.

CHAPTER 20

Adieu to a Prolific Icon

In France and around the world, the image of La Grande Mademoiselle grew to spectacular heights, culminating in an unstoppable avalanche of creative dominance. In the words of French critic, Maurice Sachs: "Coco Chanel's influence went beyond the reach of her work. Her name was etched on minds in the same way as the names of personages prominent in politics or letters. She represented, in sum, a new being."

While genius is supposed to be a gift from the Gods, usually there is a penalty attached to this gift. In Mademoiselle's case it was the absence of longtime true love. In her last days she was surfeited with fame, but lived alone and lonely. Success, however, meant financial problems were minimal. Yet, in spite of her incredible achievement, and without need for more, there was no letting up, and Coco continued to work with almost manic intensity.

Into her middle 80's and increasingly fragile, with her fingers swollen and aching, she soldiered on, producing line after acclaimed line of classic clothing. Creating up to 150 garments for each line; a cigarette in one hand, scissors in the other, she continued to build each garment on a live model, pin by pin, stitch by stitch. Doing the fittings herself, sitting on the floor or kneeling on her aching knees while she checked hems and other details, she worked six days every week, year after year. Mademoiselle hated Sundays as her studio was closed that one day of the week. It was on a Sunday in January 1971, at age 88, that years of cigarette smoking caught up with her; her heart failed and she died. Perhaps, as some suggested, if that day had been a work day she might have gone on, but in her delicate condition, the fatal Sunday would have arrived sooner or later.

While the death of Mademoiselle signified the end of an important era of fashion history, for me it brought back, along with sadness, many memories of that historic time: the pleasure of working with her and of being part of that important creative experience so vital to her successful return.

CHAPTER 21

After the Showroom Doors Open

O nce my work at the Chanel showroom was finished and my association with Tom Lee at an end, direct contact with Mademoiselle ceased. But as I stated earlier, it was comparatively easy to keep track of her activities. In the years that ensued, she continued to be very much in the news, not only in the fashion press, but in all kinds of media. Almost every achievement and skeleton in her closet has been examined, evaluated, and judged. Absent from this chatter, however, is scarcely a whisper about the Chanel Perfume Showroom in New York, and that is exactly how Coco Chanel wanted it.

As soon as she regained her rightful place as the Queen of Couture, there was no mention of her New York experience. Coco did not want to discuss the war years or her time in Switzerland, hence, her creative work in the showroom that took place following her exile was not discussed either. If the Chanel Perfume Showroom has been referred to at all, it is because of the two-page spread in *Vogue* magazine, August 15, 1953, that featured photographs of the installations and correctly credited Mademoiselle with supervising every detail. Other than that, the essential Coco Chanel creative ambiance of that no longer extant showroom is never mentioned. It is somewhat puzzling that no biographer has ever discussed her creative work in the showroom; probably because Coco never spoke of it, and the New York showroom was unknown in France.

It was different for me; throughout my working career, and even more so since I retired, the reality of my strange interlude of work with Mademoiselle loomed large in my psyche. Working with an acknowledged genius was a rare privilege. When that larger-than-life person went on to bigger and better things, to a degree, as a result of work that I was a part of, it became a fixation to follow up on Mademoiselle's continuing career. At first, I took mental notes, but as time went by I accumulated information, especially relating to her return to fame. As I knew something about her way of doing things, I was often able to read between the lines of various reports, particularly since her demise. The original trickle of material about her continued to grow: plays, movies, TV specials, over 35 books, and a cascade of articles came flooding in.

Early on, my continuing friendship with Hillel Bernstein was instrumental in acquiring background information about the workings of the French government, assorted trade organizations, and the parade of personalities involved. To clarify some of the reported happenings, I chatted occasionally with my mentor Gregory Thomas. Always a source of information, Thomas maintained his eminence in the world of fragrance until 1973, when he retired after 32 years with Chanel Perfumes. Evidently, the fine wines counteracted the chain-smoked Gauloise as he lived to 82. Tom Lee's brilliant career was unfortunately cut short at age 61 by an automobile accident. Pierre Wertheimer, having restored Chanel Perfumes to their former glory, and Chanel Couture to new heights, remained a prominent figure in the French sporting world. Seventy-six at the time of his death in 1965, he owned one of the most famous racing stables in France.

When the showroom project ended I returned to my main strength, sales promotion, continuing my work for Revlon, the United States Lines, several textile companies, and other clients. Although Revlon was considered one of the most difficult companies to deal with, during my five-year tenure, they never once complained about my work. Finally, I achieved a long sought goal: I was hired by the prestigious advertising agency, BBD&O (Batten, Barton, Durstine & Osborne), as an account executive on the Dupont account. That looked like a long term solution for career stability, until in 1960, textile giant J. P. Stevens made me an offer I could not refuse—where both my promotion and advertising experience came into play.

Stevens challenged me to create an advertising and promotional campaign tying in a Stevens slack fabric with the National Football League. Instead of the petite Mademoiselle, my partner in this TV-oriented promotion was massive All-Pro linebacker of the New York Giants, the hard working and very capable, Sam Huff. This highly profitable campaign for Stevens ran for seven years. Next came movie tie-ins for Stevens fabrics with the Warner Brothers movies, *Camelot* and *Finian's Rainbow*. Later, Warner Brothers invited me to join them at their 50th anniversary celebration at the Cannes Film Festival.

At Stevens, I was also in charge of fashion fabric advertising for both men's and women's wear, created a textile dictionary, produced Broadway-style musical fashion shows for retail audiences at major trade shows, and at one point, I was on the Board of Directors of the *Men's Fashion Association* and of the trade organization, *Woolens and Worsteds of America, Inc.* I ended my career with a return to the ad agency business, at Bozell International, working on Lee Jeans and the American Association of Railroads, before taking early retirement in 1981.

During my career and beyond, my time working with Coco Chanel, while not in the forefront of my daily existence, was always there as a kind of balance to whatever was happening. Throughout this time I continued to collect information about Mademoiselle.

I feel fortunate that the satisfaction of this interest, combined with my unique personal perspective on a pivotal episode of Coco Chanel's life, has culminated in this writing. As a surviving witness to Mademoiselle's return to fame through the vehicle of the New York Chanel Perfume Showroom, I feel privileged to add my experience, as one who knew and worked with her, to the real story behind *The Improbable Return of Coco Chanel*.

PART II

More Chanel: Myths, Legends and Lies

More Chanel presents incidents in the life of Mademoiselle Chanel that I was not part of, but which have been ignored, distorted, or fabricated by other biographers. *Sixty years of research and personal experience seek to set the record straight.*

Introduction

With the comeback of Coco Chanel securely in place, even her old antagonist, the administration of General De Gaulle, joined the "all-is-forgiven" party. The resistance hero Andre Malraux, President de Gaulle's longtime cultural minister, nominated Coco Chanel as one of the three most important people in France in the 20th century; the wife of another President, Madame Pompidou, not only wore Chanel garments, but invited Coco to have dinner at the Elysee Palace. The chief of police of Paris spoke glowingly of her. In general, her achievements were celebrated and negatives overlooked. In fact it was somewhat dangerous to criticize her in her late years, as she could more than hold her own in any discussion.

Since her death, the anti-Coco chorus is back, as virulent as it was at the time of her first, failed return. It is safe once again for misogynists to go after this upstart female any way they can. Surprisingly, much of today's anti-Coco witch hunt is perpetuated by women. Now that women's rights, pioneered by Mademoiselle, are firmly in place, the idea that this child of poverty and illegitimate parentage could rise up against bitter opposition to become a supreme tastemaker, must gall those of upscale cultural backgrounds. Probably most irked are Coco Chanel's accusers who have not achieved anywhere near the level of her success. And so they attack. After all, Mademoiselle is not here to defend herself; so it's open season.

After I finished my memoir, I felt a need to provide additional information about events in the life of Mademoiselle that have been misrepresented or even lied about. Even though I was no longer personally involved with Mademoiselle, *More Chanel* is the culmination of over 60 years of study and communication with those connected with her and with the politics of the fashion world.

It was not easy to discover the real story; Coco Chanel shielded her past with convenient myths. Anything unfavorable about her life was ignored by her or disguised through woven embellishments. Some stories are common currency, neither true nor untrue: legends created from scraps of the truth. These have been seized upon, some with positive commentary, but the majority of the retellings are absolutely absurd. In *More Chanel* I refute popular misconceptions about Coco Chanel that have been in vogue historically. Other accusations, repeated so many times that they exude the aura of truth, I have exposed as nonsense, and those can now be sent off to the abattoir for old canards.

CHAPTER 22

The Orphanage and the Church -
Where Did Coco Stand?

By the 1920s the secularization of France was ongoing; even the Catholic orphanage, haven to young Coco, was closed. Mademoiselle infrequently attended religious services and otherwise did not follow prescribed ways of living. It was assumed by her life style, that even if Coco was not against the church, she was not for it. This supposed dislike of ecclesiastical matters was bolstered by her evasion of the true facts of her childhood. In any discussion of her early days, instead of disclosing that she had been brought up by nuns in a charity orphanage, she would always say she was raised by "elderly aunts." Some thought this deception on Coco's part revealed a dislike for the nuns who ran the orphanage and a disdain for the Catholic Church.

That she sometimes referred to the "aunts" as "kindly" tells us something different. Remember, Coco lived at a time of iron clad class distinctions. Cartier, the famous jeweler, was not allowed through a client's front door; he had to use the servant's entrance. When Coco was in the company of, or having affairs with, the ultra-rich, titled, or otherwise famous, the fact that she was an illegitimate child born into poverty and brought up by charity organizations, was not a subject Coco would ever want to discuss. Hence, the nuns became "elderly aunts," a myth Coco maintained her entire life.

In 1928, Mademoiselle, at 45, creatively successful and very wealthy, gave herself a present. She built, and paid for, a luxurious retreat: a villa in the South of France so architecturally outstanding, it virtually founded a school of design philosophy. Situated in an ancient olive grove, with an extraordinary view overlooking the Mediterranean, it was a place of beauty, serenity, and sensual comfort—far from the pressures of the business world. Exterior walls and even interior ones were whitewashed, and decorations sparse, reminding visitors of the austere beauty of medieval churches. This was not a coincidence. Chanel had advised her architect, for inspiration, to visit a convent where as a child she had spent marvelous vacations. It was the 12th century Cistercian Abbey at Aubazine that housed the orphanage where she had spent so many formative years.

Perhaps Coco recognized her career was owed to the nuns; they instilled in her a passion for cleanliness, a fierce discipline, and a work ethic she retained all her life. Further, the nuns not only taught her to sew, but it appears that a probable influence to her couture esthetic evolved from the constant association with them. The fabric of their gowns hung loosely from the shoulders and moved freely, as did much of Chanel's high fashion. In a way, Coco never left the orphanage. Every evening she departed from the luxurious surroundings of her opulent apartment at 31 Rue Cambon and walked across the street to the Ritz where she slept in a very plain, small room.

In the end, Coco Chanel greatly surpassed what could have been her destiny. An unlikely beginning of life as an impoverished child in remote and rural Aubazine, ended with a splendid funeral in Paris—that highly sophisticated center of French culture. Attended by politicians, society people and notables of the fashion world, it took place at l'Eglise de la Madeleine, the church of the forgiven sinner, Mary Magdalene. Just before the service started, elegant models, dressed in Chanel's latest creations, walked slowly to reserved seats in the front rows of the church. It was a suitable farewell to the person from "nowhere," who had regained respect and opened up the world for women.

CHAPTER 23

Boy Capel, Coco Chanel's
Most Passionate Romance

One of the enduring legends of Coco Chanel is that of her adoration of Boy Capel and how sorrow over her lost love for Boy created "the *Little Black Dress*." Although his emotional and financial support allowed her entry into the world of haute couture, getting there was not easy. Before she was able to walk through the doorway he provided, she needed a lot of assistance. In France, in the years before World War I, it was almost impossible for a woman to start a business. Talented as she was, Chanel needed help—fortunately, someone was there.

After leaving the orphanage and graduating from a charity school, she had a "going nowhere" job as a tailor's assistant. The shop, in the small town of Molins, catered to officers stationed nearby. Coco helped create the glittering uniforms favored by aristocratic military, including Etienne Balsan, an army officer and wealthy estate owner. About to retire from the army, Balsan noticed Coco's talent, enjoyed her quick mind, and finding her striking beauty irresistible, asked her to join him in his retirement. That the celebrated and curvaceous beauty, Emilienne d' Alencon, was already his mistress did not impede an invitation to young Chanel. Balsan welcomed her as a charming and witty addition to his retirement life.

Moving to Balsan's estate, Royaleau, a place devoted to horses and horsemanship, Coco, as a new member of the entourage, was relegated to a room over the stables. Living in this world of equestrianism, she decided to become a significant player. Obtaining a discarded jockey's uniform, she cut it down to fit, and began to ride, astride. This was a new concept, unheard of at a time when if women rode horses at all, they rode side-saddle, wearing long, full skirts. Without planning it, Coco Chanel had created a timeless fashion innovation. Today, a hundred years later, most equestriennes dress as Coco did, in jodhpurs (fitted riding pants), and man-tailored shirts. It was Coco's first appropriation of menswear for women, a concept that would occur throughout her career. Coco rode well, cut a dashing figure, and soon moved up in the hierarchy of the estate and into the chateau. Her predecessor, Emilienne d' Alencon, moving on to better things, maintained a friendship with Coco.

It was a heady time for young Chanel, with rounds of parties and festivities. There were excursions to other mansions and often to race tracks, as racing and horses were the foci of estate living. She did have time for herself though, and her destiny as a clothing designer commenced – beginning with hats. Made from straw, simply and beautifully designed, Coco's creations were completely opposite from the heavy, overpowering millinery concoctions then in fashion. She sold her hats by wearing them, particularly at the race tracks that Balsan and his group frequented. It was not a difficult life; Coco's hats were selling well, she was treated kindly by Balsan, and accepted by his family. However, as luxurious as life was, it did not satisfy the creativity burning inside her.

Fulfillment of her dream arrived with a visiting friend of Balsan, a dark and handsome, young Englishman, Arthur Capel (called Boy). He was intrigued by this talented and beautiful young creature, and Chanel by him. It was the proverbial love at first sight for both. Chanel was attracted, not only to his looks, but to his intelligence. While most of Balsan's friends were amused only by horses, Capel, a daring and skillful polo player, shared a wide range of interests with her. Mystical insights and poems about Hindu gods, as well as his close connections with events happening in Paris and the world, captivated Coco.

At that time, aristocrats did not work. The term "idle rich," meant exactly that. In France, in spite of various revolutions and defeat by the Prussians, the rich remained leisured. In England, the worst thing you could say about anyone in the upper class was that a person was "in trade." Those who worked did not mention it; Boy Capel not only worked, he made no secret of it. Although his background was dubious, with rumors of possible illegitimate birth, the investment of his mother's family in Newcastle coal kept him busy in both France and England. It would lead to his ascendance to power in the coming war. His involvement in business was looked upon with amusement by his aristocratic friends, but was overlooked as long as he succeeded in polo and with women.

Chanel had long wanted to open a milliner's shop in Paris. And while Balsan was against this, Boy thought it had merit. That was enough for Coco to make up her mind to leave. So, in 1910 at the age of twenty-seven, with Balsan's reluctant approval, Coco and Boy, a year older than Coco, set off. As a parting gift, Ettiene Balsan loaned Coco his Paris apartment to use as a shop; financial help from Boy paid expenses.

For Coco, leaving Royaleau was not without regrets. Etienne Balsan had rescued her from oblivion, treated her with generosity, and let her pursue her first creative venture: hat making. Even though he had misgivings about Capel, he was letting her go off to Paris with him. Balsan's family had hoped that Coco and Etienne would eventually marry; and when Etienne's brother Jacques heard she was leaving, he became concerned about her future. He proffered family jewels as a means of support in case things did not work out. In reply, Coco, who had received no monetary reward, except for jewelry, during her time with Balsan, not only refused to accept Jacques' gift, but returned almost all of the jewelry Etienne had given her. She kept only an amethyst ring, which she wore on a chain around her neck for the rest of her life.

Although never faithful, Boy Capel continued to help Coco financially: first with a letter of credit, and later with the rent for a small shop on the Rue Cambon. As time went by, her business flourished in season, but she found it slow going when Paris emptied out for the summer. To follow her clients, she eventually opened a branch in Deauville, the cosmopolitan seaside resort frequented by people with money. This was a wise decision, as it was there that she made her big move, from hats into the grander world of haute couture.

When World War I broke out, the rich left Deauville and returned to Paris. Most local shops closed, and Coco was devastated. She was sure the war would destroy her new and booming business. However, as Paris came within the range of German artillery, many of the wealthy, particularly the wives, headed back to Deauville and other resorts. Unfortunately, they were not dressed for either the resorts or the war effort. As a holdover from the Belle Epoch, women of wealth wore, in addition to heavy hats, cumbersome clothing. Confined by garments that were girdled and corseted prisons, they were so weighted down by these clothes, that unassisted, they could not even step up on a curb, much less lead any kind of active life.

With most men off to the front or running war industries, women suddenly became free from social restrictions and able to participate in the war effort. Their clothes were a major hindrance—until Coco invented sportswear. Even before the war started, she advocated lightweight, easy-to-wear separates that appealed to style-conscious women. Modeling them herself as she did her hats, Coco soon had a significant following. The effects of the war, initially feared, helped create her success. From then on, Coco Chanel achieved spectacular fame and undreamed riches of a kind never before earned by a woman on her own.

As soon as she was financially able, Chanel repaid Boy Capel for the money he had advanced. At this point he is reported to have said, "I thought I was giving you a plaything; what I gave you was your freedom." He was absolutely right; never again would she accept financial help from any man. In fact, it was often the other way around; Coco Chanel rode the crest of a wave that swept her to breathtaking heights.

Meanwhile, the war raged on. In their early push, the Germans invaded neutral Belgium, surged through the undefended border, and took over the French coal mines. Boy Capel, due to connections, was made lieutenant, later captain, and put in charge of making sure that English coal was shared with France. Normally hard-working, Boy was even more industrious and became an important cog in the Allied war effort. He had enjoyed a peacetime friendship with Clemenceau, the Premier of France, and then developed an equally influential, wartime relationship with Lloyd George, the British Prime Minister.

When the war ended, Boy was famous and prosperous. He wanted to ensure his place in the world by making the right marriage. Young Coco, the bright, charming, talented French girl whom he otherwise loved, was not in the running. Coco's humble background made an official union out of the question.

After the desperate, gloomy days of war, the twenties came in with a roar, and Chanel became the epitome of the young, reckless, and daring generation. Women of the world had done well at men's work while men were in the military. For many, there was no going back to the sheltered, overdressed, subservient ways of the past. The Chanel look was everywhere. The embodiment of the 1920s, the *Flapper*, was a way of life that was all Chanel, all the way. Everything she created soared into smashing success after success. Missing almost completely from the thrill of triumph for Coco, was the one who helped get her started, and the one who still meant the most to her, Boy Capel—except occasionally.

Boy had found a useful match in an attractive, young English aristocrat, Diana Lister Wyndham, daughter of Lord Ribblesdale, and a war widow. Marrying into this prominent family would put an end to speculation about his background. Coco was resigned to the fact that marriage with Boy was an impossibility, but hoped they would still have time together. In just such a scenario, on December 24, 1919, Boy stopped off to see Coco on his way to the south of France. It was to be his last visit.

In the raging post-war years, powerful cars and fast driving were a craze among the young and wealthy, and Boy was no exception. His new high-powered convertible was in synch with his dashing style at polo and life in general. After being with Coco, he roared off to Cannes to join his pregnant wife. He did not make it. On the way, a tire blew; the car crashed and burst into flames. Boy was killed, his body burnt beyond recognition. Coco was beyond consolation. She was, she felt, the true widow, and continued to grieve. Eventually, it was said, she created the *Little Black Dress* to ensure that the world mourned with her.

CHAPTER 24

The *Little Black Dress*

In the foreseeable future, Coco Chanel will continue to be known for her inimitable perfumes, which may never be surpassed or even equaled. In the couture world, Coco Chanel is best known for elegant suits. Made from choice fabrics, impeccably tailored, incredibly constructed, always in style, they are never discarded, but end their "lives" as heirlooms or in costume collections as objects of veneration.

But, Coco Chanel's living memorial is the *Little Black Dress*. Like her fabulous perfumes, the *Little Black Dress* not only lives on, but its fashion impact continues to grow, usually with a nod to Coco, but sometimes not. The photo of Audrey Hepburn wearing a simple black Givenchy from the 1961 movie, *Breakfast at Tiffany's,* is often credited for the popularization of the *Little Black Dress*. While Audrey Hepburn was a most alluring star and Givenchy a celebrated designer, the dress she is wearing is a *long* black dress, appropriate only for evening wear. (Unless one is a call girl, like Hepburn's character, *Holly Golightly*.)

Actually, the original *Little Black Dress*, suitable for both afternoons and evenings, was created many years before Hepburn and Givenchy. In 1925, the fabulous Art Deco Exhibition in Paris featured a unique take on decorative arts and architecture. It also revealed a new concept in fashion. Pared down and sleek like the furniture and objects d'art were dresses by Chanel. Among these was a garment that became the hit of the exhibition: Coco Chanel's *Little Black Dress*.

Short in length for those days, the hem fell just below the knees. The fabric was a lightweight chiffon that hung straight down from the shoulders without much of a waistline. This seemingly simple garment set off with jewelry, usually pearls, went far to enhance the beauty of the wearer. Not merely a new style, this novel way of dressing became a sort of uniform for women of taste. To answer the question of why women would wear a somewhat impersonal dress of almost universal style, *Vogue* magazine compared it to something as equally impersonal as an automobile. "Chanel," *Vogue* said, "had created a Ford," referring to the mass-produced Ford Model T, a car that was simple, inexpensive and sold well. To complete the analogy, Henry Ford, to keep things simple, famously said "you could have any color Ford you wanted, as long as you wanted black." For years, 'ford' was a term used in the fashion world to describe a garment that was simple, stylish, and sold well, although not necessarily black.

The *Little Black Dress* exemplifies Coco's credo, "Fashion passes, style remains." This simple dress created a revolution that remains a fail-safe, timeless answer to the question of what to wear on any afternoon or evening in almost every circumstance. An indispensable travel stand-by, *Travelsmith* also recommends it for when you arrive, "Leaving you prepared for any occasion, anywhere in the world." Year after year, fashion authorities bring back the *Little Black Dress* and reinterpret it in many varieties as their inspiration for that particular season.

Not just an article of clothing, the *Little Black Dress* is an icon of measurement for anything that is smart, simple and black. Otherwise known as LBD, it has a life of its own. For example, vintners say that a wine called *Little Black Dress*, with "black cherries and elegant chocolate, make a cabernet that's timeless." They go on to say, "Like your little black dress, responsible drinking never goes out of style." The LBD has been the subject of many cartoons. In *The New Yorker*, a young woman is about to throw her dress into a blazing fire. The caption is: *"I'm burning my little black dress and moving upstate."* In the daily newspaper cartoons, when Garfield's nebbish owner finds out that his girlfriend is going to be wearing a little black dress on their date, he faints dead away. And so it goes, like the mentions of Coco herself, the references to LBD are continuous. The difference today is that Mademoiselle's reputation is frequently besmirched, while the often anonymous *Little Black Dress* continues to garner applause.

Though many people, including some in the fashion world, have forgotten who created the *Little Black Dress* and why, the legend, or perhaps the reality, reminds us that its origination was in memory of Coco's great loss, her true love, Boy Capel. The power of this legend, and the dress created by it, is so strong that eighty-seven years later, women everywhere grieve with Coco Chanel, although they know little of her love and loss.

CHAPTER 25

A Coco Legacy:
Pearls Need Not Come From Oysters

Coco Chanel had an edge over other couturiers: she was able to wear her own creations, and usually did. The simple meals of the orphanage influenced her Spartan diet, and she remained model-size all her life. Most other female dress designers, while stylish enough, were not of the right dimensions to wear their own creations to advantage. Coco was one of the most photographed celebrities of her time, and as she always wore something new and newsworthy, she soon had a following of young women who wanted to look like her. Coco loved that and encouraged them to imitate her style. She once said, "There are forty thousand little dressmakers in France. Where can they find their ideas, if not from us? Let them copy. I am on the side of women and seamstresses, not the fashion houses."

Coco's openness to being copied led her to resign from the Chambre Syndicale de la Couture Parisienne, an organization in Paris created to prevent piracy of couture design, in part by prohibiting photography at openings. Coco objected to this imposed secrecy and invited photographers to showings. She really wanted her garments copied openly, knowing no matter how hard anyone, or any organization, tried to protect ideas, knock-offs were a tradition impossible to control. And besides, imitation is a sincere form of flattery. Her accessories were another story, particularly her innovative jewelry. At first it was not possible for anyone to reproduce her impressive originals because they were frightfully expensive, and the costume jewelry industry did not exist. Until she created it.

After the Grand Duke of Imperial Russia, Dmitri Pavlovich, escaped to France during the Russian Revolution, he and Coco had an ardent affair. Tall, handsome Dmitri and much shorter, but beautifully put together, Coco, made an enthralling pair—her glamour enhanced by the ropes of Romanoff pearls he gave her. From then on Coco was rarely without pearls and that became a signature, rather like the perfume she always wore.

However, the average person could not afford natural pearls, their rich beauty harvested from the sea at great cost. To allow a more complete copy of her style, she had artisans create artificial pearls; Coco then launched the style of wearing long strands of pearls, either real or artificial, depending upon your pocketbook. Similarly, in her usual innovative way, Coco used one of the first synthetic plastics, Galalith, extensively for buttons and garment trimmings. An imitation ivory that looked strikingly real, Galalith became a staple in the Art Deco jewelry industry.

In the 1920s as a fashion first, Coco wore glittering jewelry, typically reserved for the evening, throughout the day. Coco's follow-up with defiantly fake costume jewelry scored high with the extravagant set; imitation pearls and other faux jewelry she commissioned became a fixture of cafe society and the bourgeoisie. In the not-so-glittering thirties, she was asked by the authentic jewelry industry to create new designs using real jewels. For this she relied on titled artisans like Count Etienne de Beaumont to create objects of extraordinary beauty. And Coco created a star in the world of exotic jewelry when she asked Sicilian Duke Fulco di Vedura to create specific jewelry to compliment certain of her garments, the first couturier to do so. His clunky metal bracelets worn on both wrists became a classic look. It did not bother Coco that these were quickly knocked off by the costume jewelry industry, an industry Coco helped to create. The knock-off still goes on, and the enormous costume jewelry industry of today owes much to Coco Chanel.

CHAPTER 26

The Mystique of Chanel Perfumes

My involvement with the enlarged N°5 bottle stopper (used as a door handle in the Chanel Perfume Showroom), triggered my curiosity about the story behind the creation of this fabulous fragrance. After many conversations with those in the know, both at the Chanel office and the trade press, particularly *Women's Wear Daily,* I sorted out the complex story of how Number 5, despite its high cost, became the best-selling perfume in the world. According to what I learned, the long running Chanel perfume saga began in 1924. As mentioned earlier, buoyed by her success in the world of couture, Coco explored the idea of creating her own fragrance. Perfume by couturiers was not a new idea; most of the main houses had several offerings. Even today, someone no sooner comes out with a successful line of apparel, or has fifteen minutes of fame than they follow that success with a perfume or two. These, in turn, usually have their own fifteen minutes of fame, before quietly fading away. Recent examples include the TV show, *Desperate Housewives*; starlet Hilary Duff, and celebrities Paris Hilton, Britney Spears, and the teen idol, Taylor Swift.

One of Mademoiselle's credos was that a woman without

the right perfume was not properly dressed, but Coco was un-happy because she could not find one that really pleased her. With typical Chanel bravura, she decided not only to create a signature fragrance, but to concoct the best perfume ever made, and add a most important element: elegance that lasted. To de-vise a fragrance she herself would like, Coco turned to her one-time lover, the former Grand Duke Dimitri of Russia, for help. After World War I, with the Russian Revolution triumphant, the Grand Duke no longer had a country. However, Dimitri still had influence, and he remained her friend. To help her gain entrée to the perfume industry, he introduced Coco to Ernest Beaux, a chemist, who knew a great deal about fine fragrances. His father had been the head perfumer to the court of the Tsar.

Growing up in the world of extravagant perfumes of the Imperial Russian Court, Beaux had learned it well. During the Russian Revolution, after serving with the White Russians in bitter fighting in the frozen wastes of the north, he escaped to France. Beaux continued the family business, Perfumes Rallet, in Grasse, the main source of floral essences in France. Beaux had offered a perfume to Coty, who thought it would be too expensive to produce. When he proposed it to Coco she asked what made it so costly. Told that jasmine was the high priced ingredient, she told Beaux to add even more jasmine to her new perfume. Beaux did, and added, as requested, other costly floral essences, including patchouli, iris, rose, and flowers from the ylang ylang tree, from far off Malaysia. Create the highest de-gree of luxury and hang the expense, was Coco's approach. But even with sumptuous ingredients, the results were not right; none lasted long enough. Then Beaux, breaking with tradition, added a synthetic, aldehyde, to extend the aroma, transforming a fleeting floral scent into a blend of lasting fragrance, a perfume that not only helped a woman dress properly, but lingered with her throughout an entire evening.

Beaux worked with Coco for some time and when ready for the final decision, he lined up a row of fragrances for her to test. *Vogue* once said that Coco Chanel had perfect pitch in taste; she also possessed intensified sensory perceptions in other ways. Her sense of smell was uncommonly keen; it enabled her to dis-cern which scents would create fragrance perfection. When she tested the row of perfumes, the first four were not quite right. But when she came to the fifth sample, her acute receptivity to divergent fragrances told her this was it. The symbolism for the always superstitious Coco was overwhelming, as the number 5 was coincidently her lucky charm. And so the fifth sample became Chanel N°5, a new concept in fragrances and a novel way to name a perfume. While Ernest Beaux deservedly gets much credit for the chemistry of N°5 - the judicious blending of 80 ingredients and the addition of aldehyde and other chemicals - it was Chanel who dictated which aromatic ingredients she wanted in the perfume, as well as the famous bottle. Simple in style like the name of the perfume, it is considered a classic artifact of *Art Deco* design.

Once in her showroom, the new fragrance took off, way beyond the capacity of Beaux's ability to handle the demand. When Coco found that Beaux could not manage increased production and distribution, she asked Theophile Bader, the president of Gallery Lafayette, a major retail establishment in Paris, where to go next. He recommended the Werthheimer brothers, as they produced volume perfumes in their Bourjois line, including "*Evening In Paris.*"

In a meeting with the Wertheimers, Coco, disinterested in the arduous details of marketing a new product, turned everything over to them. This once, her usually shrewd sense of business left her. Not realizing the incredible world-wide potential of N°5, she suggested and signed a contract giving her 10% of the profit from French sales. After all, other couturiers had perfumes too, and none of them were big money makers. It was, at the time of its creation, the right thing to be involved with, a sort of fun thing to do, but it seemed a minor issue to her, in the total scheme of the world of Chanel Couture.

Pierre Wertheimer knew otherwise and was so delighted with this arrangement, that after the meeting he gave Bader, who had done nothing more than introduce Chanel to the Wertheimers, 20% of the profits for France. That the Wertheimers knew a good thing when they smelled it was obvious, and very fortuitous for their heirs. Today, *Evening in Paris*, then Bourjois' main perfume, barely exists, while Chanel perfumes look as if they will go on forever.

For a while, however, the future of Chanel Perfumes was clouded by Coco's animosity toward the Wertheimers, particularly during the years of her exile. Without work and eventually without love, with nothing else in life to interest her, hating the Wertheimers (even though it was her own mistake), and seeking revenge became her only outlet. Suit after suit followed until Pierre Wertheimer decided his need for her personal touch was far greater than the financial cost she had been suing for. It was a long shot. His gamble on the publicity benefits from her resurrection into a primary celebrity was not a certainty. It was entirely based on the public relations benefit that could accrue from her creative approach to the new Chanel Perfume Showroom.

CHAPTER 27

Chanel Promotes a Healthy Sun Tan

It is accepted today that a tan looks good and is healthful. It was not always so. As the waning years of the Belle Epoch lingered into the 20th century, European aristocracy, and those who aspired to it, openly displayed the difference between the classes through their skin color. The dead-white skin of the gentry instantly identified them as the idle rich, for whom no gainful employment was allowed. People who worked, whether in the fields, in trades or manual labor, had healthy tans just from being out-of-doors. Any possibility of exposure to the sun for the elite warranted a complete cover-up: wide-brimmed hats for men and women, supplemented by parasols for females, was the order of the day. To have skin as white as possible was a core value among the wealthy, albeit a most dangerous assumption. Unfortunately, the health and longevity of the upper class suffered from this almost complete lack of vitamin D, the essential vitamin that comes naturally from the sun.

A change in the criteria of skin tone as a measure of class distinction came about when Coco Chanel, after liberating women from cumbersome clothing through her invention of sportswear, promoted outdoor living for them as well. A natural tan, as part of this new look, became an integral part of this fashion statement. It was something everyone could achieve; after all, sunshine was free. Because of Coco's innovation, healthy tans became the way of life for all classes, regardless of background. Social distinctions by skin color in European society ended, and it has become hard to tell the debutante from the shop girl.

Although never mentioned in the outpouring of information on the benefits of vitamin D from sunshine, Coco Chanel's incredible instincts led her to create the vogue for healthy tans - long before scientific evidence recommended them.

CHAPTER 28

Coco, Unconscious Mentor to the Flapper Generation

The upheaval caused by World War I set the stage for a dramatic change in the way the Western world worked, especially for women. By the war's end they competed with men in business and even in the political world, obtaining, at least to some degree, social and financial independence. These "new" women wanted a change from the oppressive regulations of the Victorian era. They were ready to overthrow restrictive rules that dictated the way they dressed and acted; above all, they wanted to pursue a life style that would be in keeping with their new freedom. Coco Chanel, through her life's example, showed them the way.

At the Art Deco exhibition of 1924, in Paris, the *Little Black Dress* was the hit of the show, but other garments by Chanel were just as popular. Paving the way for a complete revolution in the way women dressed and lived, Coco's invention of sportswear, allowed women to participate in an active life. To top it off, she showed how to have a successful career in business as well as fashion.

The transition to the new woman was enhanced by the media attention showered on Coco. Constantly in the news, photographed with one famous person after another and always seen in her latest fashions, she enjoyed celebrity status and her standing as a mentor. Not shy about her leadership, Coco proclaimed she was *"The first to live the life of this century!"*

In America the *New Women* were called *Flappers*. Like Coco, they wore short skirts, dispensed with corsets, affected a slim boyish look, bobbed their hair, drank and smoked in public, and pursued an active life. Exulting in this new found freedom, they danced the night away to the Charleston and other jazz favorites. While the word "Flapper" was seldom applied to Coco, they owed almost everything to her—even though Coco Chanel was known to most of them by name only.

CHAPTER 29

The Two Richest People in Europe

Coco Chanel's great love for Boy Capel, an upward striver with somewhat dubious credentials was not returned by him with the same intensity. As written earlier, as beautiful and talented as she was, this little peasant from an unlikely background was not the suitable mate Boy Capel needed. That woman had to be someone of means and impeccable qualifications.

Some years later, when the very wealthy and socially prominent Hugh Richard Arthur Grosvenor, the Duke of Westminster, met Mademoiselle Chanel, his reaction was different. He was fascinated not only with her style and beauty, but with her accomplishments. An international celebrity, she was a successful business woman, first creating and then running Chanel Couture—a financial empire of salons, workshops and textile mills. Then there was the jewelry, other accessories, and her creation of famous perfumes, including the legendary N°5. Incredible achievements, almost entirely through her own efforts.

While the Duke was the richest man in England, his enormous wealth, almost entirely inherited, did not take up much of his time; his estate was entirely handled by financial managers. Living in the world of the idle rich, he had never met a woman like Coco, and he wanted to know her better. The Duke went by the nickname *Bendor*, a moniker given to him by his father, who gave the same name to his favorite horse. A not unusual combination: in aristocratic circles, a prize winning horse was often favored over members of the family, as was also the case with the Wertheimer family.

The Duke of Westminster's inheritance included vast amounts of London real estate which allowed him to feel superior to the Royal Family. Bendor had more wealth and his heritage went back further than theirs. No fashion plate, he dressed as he wished without regard to social convention and with certain eccentricities. While his valet ironed his shoe laces every night, the shoes themselves were patched and otherwise repaired; he did not wish to give up the comfort provided by these elderly boots, and of course, no one would dare criticize his wardrobe. In his relationships with people he often had problems, as he could be overly imperious. He made up for it though, by giving generous rewards to the people around him. Noted for casual liaisons, although a recent one had caused a scandal that led to an acrimonious divorce, the Duke was looking for a permanent relationship with someone who could stand up to him. Coco Chanel seemed to be that person.

But Coco was of another world and very wealthy herself; the Duke and his riches were not of interest to her. He tried sending her out-of-season fruits and vegetables from his greenhouses; when that got no response he sent a basket of produce that included a giant emerald hidden among the vegetables. Finally, with the prompting of her friend and ex-lover, Grand Duke Dimitri, a cousin to Bendor, she consented to visit him.

Meeting on one of Bendor's yachts, a converted destroyer with a crew of 180, they enjoyed being together and later embarked on a cruise. This first cruise was not smooth sailing, but the Duke was impressed with her ability to weather rough seas. From then on they were together, on and off, for ten years. To ensure her own comfort, she designed slacks that made shipboard life more enjoyable. Sometimes they sailed on one of his yachts, or stayed at one of his palatial homes in England, or at her vacation home in the South of France, where a special suite was created for him. Always, without interruption, she continued to maintain her couture empire, designing 150 garments by hand, for each of two showings a year. Bendor was impressed by her work ethic; he had never known anyone like her.

The time spent at his estate was profitable for her, as she now added many items from Bendor's closet to her couture designs. She converted jackets, ties, sweaters - all in menswear styling - into typical Chanel wearable styles for women. Bendor and Coco, as a couple, were popular in England with the daily press and even among aristocrats. This was a far cry from France, where people who worked were put in their place. From the favorable reception Coco enjoyed, she gained a liking for English people and products, including tweeds, which became one of her favorite fabrics.

The Duke had inherited a gallery of paintings by noted artists, including Reynolds, Rubens, Raphael, Hals, Goya, Valazquez, and others of the same prominence, but when Coco introduced him to her friends in the creative world, he was not impressed. Perhaps just owning great art does not necessarily make you an art lover, particularly when the collection is inherited. Some in England were shocked when the Duke sold Gainsborough's "Blue Boy" to the American, Henry Huntington. But Gainsborough was not an aristocrat and the model was just a local boy dressed up in fancy clothing. Why bother keeping the painting around, particularly when you are offered a lot of money for something you don't feel akin to?

The chances of the Duke having a relationship with someone from as poverty-stricken a background as Coco would have been impossible if Bendor had known the details of her early years. Coco made sure he did not; discussions of her past life were quickly terminated. Like Winston Churchill and other English aristocrats, the Duke spoke excellent French, making conversation easy for her. As long as they stuck to safe ground they generally got on well.

Bendor occasionally went back to his wayward days. When Coco found out about one of his indiscretions, she let him know she was aware of it. While Boy was never faithful, his support was essential to her early success and his lapses were ignored, but she owed nothing to the Duke. When Bendor realized Coco was on to his latest misadventure, he knew he had to make up for his transgression. Armed with a suitable gift, he invited her to one of his yachts. Coco agreed to visit and after embarking she waited, standing by the rail with her hands extended over it. Bendor approached, and after greeting her, slipped into her hands a stunning emerald. To show how little things of monetary value meant to her, she opened her hands and let the precious jewel slide into the water.

The relationship did not improve. A basic problem was the Duke's need for a male heir. His only son had died young and as only males could inherit in England, unless he had a male child, his much disliked nephew would inherit everything. Now in her mid 40's, Coco was not able to conceive; the relationship fell apart and Bendor married a much younger woman. Ironically, she was not able to supply an heir and the inheritance eventually went to the hated nephew.

As far as the breakup was concerned, Coco's insatiable need to work always came first, and a marriage that would seek to convert her into one of the leisured rich would never have worked. She was quoted as saying she declined the Duke's offer of marriage because, "While there have been many Duchesses of Westminster, there could only ever be one Coco Chanel."

CHAPTER 30

Courtesan or Industrial Tycoon?

The trickle of stories following Coco Chanel's return from exile has grown into a torrent, including over 25 books, a play, movies, TV documentaries, and an avalanche of articles. In spite of the amount of coverage, it is amazing how little is really known about her. Unfortunately, most of those involved in these projects neither knew her, nor the actual details of her life. Hence, there are many errors, even outright lies, reported as facts. While some of this material extols her achievements, there is usually an undercurrent of negativity. This is, I guess, the usual predisposition of the herd to bring down the maverick. And there is no question that Coco Chanel was the essential maverick from the very beginning, a rebel who defied convention.

Recently, the degrading of the image of Coco Chanel has plunged to new depths. Her positive achievements have been so divulged, over and over, that in order to find a publisher one must dig up something scandalous about her, even if it's only partially true or not true at all. Morally, she is often assailed; sometimes Coco is called a grisette (a cheap whore), or a cocotte, a little higher on the scale, but still a prostitute. Most frequently the word courtesan is used. Higher class yes, but still, Webster defines courtesan as a prostitute. *Smithsonian* magazine recently led off an article with the descriptive heading: "Couturier and courtesan, Coco made her own rules." There are many other examples of this from usually reputable media. For those who do not like the idea that women can be accomplished in business, a standard way of downgrading females who have done well, is to single them out as having gained their success through the use of sexual prowess.

In any event, as Coco Chanel is often charged with using sex to succeed, let's look at the record and at the men who had the deepest connections to her. First, consider her father, who never gave her the love she needed as a child. Coco's fragile mother died when Coco was eight; her father drifted away without saying goodbye, leaving her alone and lonely in a charity orphanage. She never heard from him again. Although this solitary emptiness stayed with her no matter how successful she became, the situation could have predisposed Coco to wanting and needing to be taken care. But did it?

It is true that after leaving the orphanage and charity school, Chanel's dim future brightened when she met and tailored the uniform of wealthy officer, Etienne Balsan. As written earlier, when he was ready to retire he asked Coco to join him at his estate. Having nowhere else to go, she did not turn him down. Without a dowry, she would have little chance of a suitable marriage and could end up like her mother, dying neglected in abject poverty.

And yes, at Balsan's estate Coco shared his opulent life, including innovative parties and exciting equestrian events. Yet in spite of the lavish financial gain marriage would have brought, Coco resisted. Although she respected Balsan, she was not in love with him, or his life style, and she had a desperate need to be independent.

If she had been a common prostitute, or even a courtesan, as many maintain, do you think she would have returned all but one piece of jewelry given to her by Balsan, or that Balsan's family would have even considered a marriage between Etienne and Coco desirable?

There was another reason for leaving the Balsan estate: Coco did not wish to spend her life in the idleness inherent in an easy-going equestrian setting. Her hat-making had set off a spark, lighting a fire that burned bright. The creative work involved cast its spell on her and Coco needed to let her talent soar. It did so when she met Boy Capel, never to die out. True, Boy Capel financed her start in the couture world, and their long drawn out affair continued even after his marriage to another woman. But by the time of his deadly accident, Coco had paid back the money he had loaned her. Not the standard practice of prostitutes.

It was not long before her couture business boomed and eventually she was the richest self-made woman in the world, almost entirely due to her own talent and effort. From then on, there were several affairs, but except for her (financially) equal-status romance with the super wealthy Duke of Westminster, all other lovers were supported by *her*. This included the composer Igor Stravinsky; the former and then impoverished Grand Duke of Russia; the poet Pierre Reveredy; the cartoonist and designer Paul Iribe; and her wartime lover, Baron von Dincklage.

From this evidence, the career path of Coco Chanel was not exactly that of a prostitute, as many, for whatever reason, allege. However, I don't think that the true story of Mademoiselle's life will keep writers, male or female, who need something - any-thing - new, from creating purely speculative embellishments or completely fictional events.

Aside from the designation of Coco Chanel as a prostitute, she is often denigrated as "just a dress designer," without regard to her achievements in opening the world to women and as an arbiter of taste. Hardly mentioned and almost unknown is the eminence Coco Chanel achieved as a business executive. In spite of its enormous size and scope, there is little understanding of the economic power of her industrial empire. Chanel Couture was, in no way, a boutique operation. Not counting those who worked for Chanel Perfumes under the management of Pierre Wertheimer, Coco Chanel employed over 4,000 people in her studios, work rooms and textile mills. She was the catalyst for the evolution of the costume jewelry industry and reinvigorated fine jewelry marketing and manufacturing through her own designs and workshops. And of course, her invention of Chanel N°5 and other fragrances created the perfume industry as we know it today.

Outside of initial help from Boy Capel, the rest of Coco Chanel's business empire grew as a result of her own merits. In her time (an era when women were supposed to be subservient to men), no other female came close to building an industrial and cultural empire that compared to the one created by Coco Chanel. In point of fact: she was not a courtesan; she was a high-ranking industrial tycoon.

Like most plutocrats, Coco was not overly concerned with the financial and emotional needs of her workers. A six-day week was normal for her, and she expected the same from her employees. In the turbulent days leading up to World War II, this attitude caught up with Coco when her employees went on strike. Coco was shocked; in her mind, working for Chanel Couture was a privilege that was more important than a five-day work week, paid vacations, or adequate salaries. Her way of running Chanel Industries with an iron fist was right out of the playbook of a classic industrial tycoon.

Almost every book, article, movie, or whatever, about Coco Chanel, brings up the phony prostitute angle or the Nazi nonsense. Surprisingly, few talk about her creation of a giant industrial empire and how she ran it. That's not sexy I guess.

CHAPTER 31

Coco Chanel's Last Love:
The Baron Hans Gunter Von Dincklage

A Spy? A Nazi?
Officer in the Dreaded SS?
A Member of the Gestapo?
Or Perhaps, None of These

I n addition to unflagging devotion to work, Coco Chanel maintained a constant search for long-lasting love, seldom with any degree of fulfillment. It began when her mother died and her father walked away. While taken in and treated well at the orphanage, it was years before she accepted the fact that she would never see her father again. And then there was her true love, Boy Capel, who abandoned her for a wealthy widow. As Coco became rich and famous there would be affairs with dukes, poets, artists, composers, and a host of other talented or titled people, but in the end, no long-lasting love.

The war offered her one last chance. When the Germans conquered France and imprisoned her nephew, she went to the enemy to try and obtain his release. Up to this point, Coco's way of handling the occupation was to ignore it. When the Nazis first occupied Paris, as part of their charm offensive, popular figures in the arts and entertainment worlds were allowed considerable freedom, as long as they were not Jewish. Couture houses continued showings of fashions, Maurice Chevalier kept on performing, and Cartier prospered, selling expensive jewelry to Herman Goering and other high-ranking Nazis. Likewise, Pablo Picasso, a very vocal communist before the war, continued to paint unmolested. Although his art was banned by Hitler, a few minor German officers even bought paintings from him. Books of a non-subversive nature were allowed to be written and published. Occupying soldiers were on their best behavior and the Nazi war machine was forging ahead and seemed to be on the way to take over the world. There was, at that time, little hope of freedom from German power and a kind of acceptance of France's status of being a lesser political entity.

Coco Chanel, an international presence and significant cultural force, was never hindered by occupation authorities. Her apartment in the Ritz was held for her; all she had to do was announce who she was and the way was cleared. Coco, however, somewhat of a chauvinist inspired by Boy Capel's exploits in World War I, had wept bitter tears when France fell. Aware of her importance to her country, she would walk past German soldiers as if they did not exist. Now needing help from the enemy, she was referred to a man she could not ignore: a tall, handsome, French-speaking, German diplomat, Baron Hans Gunter Von Dincklage, whom she had known before the War.

Suave in three languages, his excellent French was a complement to his perfect English. His mother had been of the British aristocracy and there is speculation that he might have been a double agent. Actually, he was not even a reputable one for the Germans. He originally came to Paris during the pre-war years looking for a job that offered him a lot of leisure, time necessary to become acquainted with wealthy ladies—the kind who could support him in the manner he had been accustomed.

Part of the old order in Germany, he continued working for the government, as many did when Hitler took over, but without evident enthusiasm for the new regime. Stationed in Paris, ostensibly as cultural attaché to the German embassy, his supposed job was to keep tabs on the French social world. His aristocratic background and abundance of charm suited him well for this task, particularly since he was more interested in the contents of wine cellars than in French military installations. The small income his work provided cramped his style, and he was always on the lookout for favorable financial opportunities, usually through well-to-do women. With the Nazis firmly in power, Von Dincklage ditched his far-from-wealthy wife, and remained in Paris to be away from the center of intrigue that Berlin had become. Just before the war he had gained financial support from a prosperous lady of questionable background. Regrettably, for the Baron's economic situation, but necessary for her existence, she made a timely exit from France.

The Baron was hard put to maintain his lavish life style until he became reacquainted with the very wealthy Mademoiselle Chanel. It was as if he had discovered a diamond mine. By promoting his English background, he soon made his claim secure by moving into Coco's apartment in the Ritz. The winter of 1940-1941 was the coldest in years and to make it worse, the Germans had confiscated most of the French coal. As the Baron and Coco huddled together in the remorseless cold, he strengthened his British persona by teaching her English. After her legendary affair with Boy Capel, her romance with the Duke of Westminster, and her phenomenal reception from the British people and press, Coco had a love for all things English. She considered the English-speaking Baron a version of English aristocracy, which in a way he was, as his mother was of British nobility. According to photographs, there was even a physical resemblance between the Baron and the Duke of Westminster. Similar to Coco's myth that changed the nuns of the orphanage to elderly aunts, to her, Von Dincklage was not really German—he was always English.

There was a potential problem: Coco at 58 was twelve years older than the Baron. The age difference gave her the lame excuse for a relationship with the enemy during the war. She supposedly said, "When a man, much younger than you, wants to be your lover, you don't ask to see his passport." As long as the money was there, Coco being older, did not bother the Baron. He was, in fact, just a gigolo—of the old fashioned, "Kiss Your Hand Madam" variety.

Other than marrying a nouveau riche American heiress looking for a title as a way to improve her social standing, being a gigolo was one of the few occupations available to landless, financially-impoverished, European aristocrats, like the Baron. As far as being a Nazi, or an SS officer, there was no record of him joining the party, or being in the military service. Actually, he was anti-military and hated the war, as did Coco. They often discussed their mutual dislike of the conflict and the wartime conditions inflicted on them. As the war dragged on, the Baron, to avoid responsibility of any kind, kept a low profile, staying as far away from the authorities as possible, even to the point of making sure that he and Coco were seldom seen together.

As war with Russia turned into a disaster for the Germans, Von Dincklage, concerned that he might be called up for military service on the Russian front, or sent to the absolute can of worms Berlin had become, hid out full-time in Coco's lavish apartment over her now closed atelier at 31 rue Cambon. He managed to keep out of sight until the war ended, was quickly cleared by the Allied Occupation authorities, and retired in Switzerland.

Coco, unhappy with her standing with the government of resistance hero Charles de Gaulle, joined the Baron in Switzerland. Alas, somewhere in the boredom of exile, Coco's last love affair ended. Actually, there wasn't a complete break between Coco and the Baron, as she continued to support him financially, even after they were no longer together. This finally ended when she left Switzerland for New York to become Creative Director of the new Chanel Perfume Showroom, and in the process, regained her standing as a creative genius. There was never anyone else. While love was out of the picture forever, her other key to life - work - flourished, assuming the role of her only pleasure.

CHAPTER 32

German Generals, Churchill, and the Plot to End the War

The loss of North Africa and the capture there of an elite German army, the surrender of another German army at Stalingrad, and their imprisonment in Soviet Gulags made many high ranking German officers realize that the supposed military genius, Adolph Hitler, was indeed a mad man. Facing a dismal future for Germany if taken over by the ruthless Red Army, many in the military tried to find ways to end the war. On one such occasion, bombs were set off in a room where Hitler had been, but missed him by a few minutes. Count Berthold Von Stauffenberg, one of the chief conspirers of the failed assassination attempt of 1944, was executed when the plot was discovered. There were many other attempts. Erwin Rommel, one of Germany's best generals was found to be part of such a plot. His participation in the attempt to end the war was uncovered by the SS, and he was given a death sentence. Protected by his military surroundings where he could be safe, Rommel was told if he did not commit suicide, his son would be executed. He complied.

While in hiding, Von Dincklage, who had always hated the war, apprised Coco of the hope of the German military's aristocratic leadership, that a negotiated end to the war could be achieved. Coco, who had begun to think of herself as an international figure, above politics, foolishly decided to get involved. She presumed that her friendship with Winston Churchill provided a chance to pass on the German wish for negotiated peace. Her rather involved effort was a significant misstep. Churchill, remembering the failure of the Armistice of the First World War and the quick rearmament of Germany afterward, routinely rejected such offers. Coco's effort went nowhere except into the documentation of German espionage operations.

Other accusations against her resulted from knowledge of her attempt to use Nazi race laws to regain control of Chanel Perfume from Wertheimer. But actually, that was just one of many lawsuits she had pressed against him down through the years.

On the other hand, it is interesting that Justine Picardie notes in *Coco Chanel, The Legend and the Life* that the architect of Coco's Mediterranean villa was a member of the Resistance and asked her to come there, to help him gain a friend's release from the Gestapo. She made the trip to her villa as requested, which could have been very dangerous as it was used by the Resistance as a message center, while the garden was a staging area for Jewish refugees escaping from France. As this retreat, a splendid embodiment of her own psyche, was of critical importance to her, it is inconceivable that she would not have been aware of what was happening there.

This use by the Resistance of her Riviera villa is perhaps why Andre Malraux, noted writer, Resistance leader and the Minister of Culture under her old antagonist Charles De Gaulle, was so approving of her. So, too, were the Chief of Paris Police, and the President of France, George Pompidou.

In an ironic aftermath, Winston Churchill, in his retirement, was looking for a comfortable retreat in the balmy South of France and spent much time at Coco Chanel's charming villa. Roquebrune had been purchased for him by his literary agent, Emery Reves. For many years, that remained Churchill's second home and haven from the interruptions of the political world. It was where he wrote several volumes of his memoirs. None of them included mention of Mademoiselle Chanel.

After the triumphant return of Chanel Couture and the resurgent fame of her perfumes, her affair with Von Dincklage and her attempt to end the war faded from memory. So much so, that Andre Malraux stated: "In the 20th century, the three most important people for France were *Charles de Gaulle, Pablo Picasso* and *Coco Chanel.*" This acceptance by both the business and political world continued long after her death. Lately however, with nothing new to write about, old negatives have reemerged and her accomplishments downgraded. As all things run in cycles, there may be another wave of Chanel appreciation on the horizon. Perhaps this writing will begin a fresh look at the real Coco Chanel.

CHAPTER 33

The Summing Up: A Real Puzzlement

An enigma wrapped in myths and legends, her life a captivating narrative, Coco Chanel continues to fascinate. Much about Mademoiselle is known, much is hidden. It is easy to knock her, to fabricate negatives, to turn her into nothing more than a clever dressmaker and ultimate strumpet. She is dead and anyone can make up a story out of remnants and scraps and to presume, in print, or film, that these conjectures are of whole cloth.

But the real puzzlement is: *where is the truth?* How did this peasant child from one of the poorest parts of rural France, educated only in an orphanage and charity school, become the supreme arbiter of style and fashion? How did she invent the world's finest perfumes, change the way women dress and live, and in the process, build the most important industrial complex ever created by a woman?

First, by overcoming the mind-numbing loss of her parents—a loss of heart-rending sorrow that built a protective wall which armored her against disappointment. Then while living in the orphanage, she adopted the mantra of a life-long workaholic, the nuns having inspired in her a fierce discipline. Exposed to a simple but rigorous life, she gained an unwavering belief in herself and her talents and almost always trusted her instincts. Her career was the result of the nuns teaching her to sew. And perhaps, as suggested earlier, she had been unconsciously influenced by the classic simplicity of their habits.

Be that as it may, much of her early life was not dissimilar from that of other children who lost their parents and ended up in an orphanage somewhere in France. While most of these may have graduated to meaningful lives, there was *only one Coco Chanel*. What then is the key ingredient that made her different? To appreciate this standout quality we can look to the realm of music.

To be a great star in the music world, one must have perfect pitch. But, perfect pitch cannot be learned; it must be inherited. Not everyone who has perfect pitch becomes a virtuoso; contributing factors towards becoming a successful musician include an unrelenting drive to excel and a willing sacrifice of much of your life to the demand of constant practice. Esteemed recognition in music requires both talent and hard work.

After previewing the new Chanel Perfume Showroom in New York, *Vogue's* enthusiastic report of August 15, 1953, credited its success to the fact that Coco Chanel possessed accurate taste, just as some people have perfect pitch in music. *Vogue* had it right: Mademoiselle Chanel was born with perfect pitch in taste. There were also other inborn attributes. Her sense of smell, essential to the creation of perfume, was so superior, she observed that when someone proffered cut flowers, she could distinguish the aroma of the person who had picked them.

Born with a formidable intelligence that allowed her to fit in with whatever group she was associated with, her personality sparkled in all situations. Moving to Etienne Balsan's estate, she immediately gained a starring role in the theatrical fetes so popular there. She even won the approval of Balsan's reigning mistress, Emilienne d'Alencon, who found Chanel "amusing." In spite of Coco's lack of formal education, her ability to feel comfortable with highly educated aristocrats, as well as ordinary workers, was immediate.

She was naturally charming, a trait that also aided her legendary ability to work with the press. As she aged she lost none of her ability to reach out to the media. In the 1960s, when Mademoiselle was in her eighties, Diana Vreeland of *Vogue* found her extraordinarily "alert, mesmerizing, strange, alarming, charming and witty." According to Vreeland, "just about every man who met Mademoiselle fell in love with her."

Coco Chanel's inborn attributes, combined with a powerful work ethic, a formidable belief in 'self,' and her ability to always be, not only in style, but ahead of the pack, allowed her to become in the end, and forever, La Grande Mademoiselle.

CHAPTER 34

The End of the
Chanel Perfume Showroom

Pierre Wertheimer's health declined and he died in 1965, Coco in 1971. After the death of Mademoiselle there was no one in charge at Chanel until 1974, when Alain Wertheimer, the twenty-five-year-old grandson of Pierre, moved in and took over. While Alain had never met Coco, he was a carbon copy of Pierre and soon set the company back on track. Alain built Chanel, Inc. into one of the largest luxury goods companies in the world, with estimated sales over two billion dollars. The exact figure is unknown, as he is as secretive about business as his grandfather.

Gregory Thomas retired as head of Chanel America in 1972, and was replaced by Kitty d'Alessio. She lured Karl Lagerfeld from Chloe to give pizzazz to the new ready-to-wear lines. This proved a successful move for Lagerfeld as his creations did so well he became the new star at Chanel. Known in the trade as *King Karl*, he became so powerful he succeeded in ousting D'Alessio and things changed drastically.

The Chanel showroom that spoke so eloquently of Chanel taste was not reflective of the flamboyant Lagerfeld. Consequently, the Chanel Perfume Showroom that Coco Chanel created was disassembled and the Chanel office moved to 57th street. The new showroom captured Lagerfeld's *go-go* philosophy (radically different from Coco's concepts, just as his designs are of the moment and hers were for the ages).

One remnant of the old showroom is still in use. The enlarged N°5 bottle stopper now opens the door to the current Chanel showroom. After all these years, the emerald cut, art deco handle is still an elegant and allegorical means of entrée to the wonders of the world of Chanel.

I assume that the fine art and antiques in the showroom, where Mademoiselle was the creative director, were returned to the Wertheimer family. The Coromandel screens are another story. Moving them would have been difficult as they were cut to fit existing doors and fastened to the wall. Perhaps in some storage space in the building where the Chanel showroom used to be, the screens sit idle and useless. That curator at the Metropolitan Museum of Art was right in being cautious about sending someone, no matter how experienced, to cut Coromandel...

Made in the USA
Lexington, KY
28 November 2013